AF480904

# FOOD QUALITY MANAGEMENT

## TEXTBOOK FOR UG & PG STUDENTS

DR SUNIL KUMAR

Copyright © Dr Sunil Kumar
All Rights Reserved.

This book has been self-published with all reasonable efforts taken to make the material error-free by the author. No part of this book shall be used, reproduced in any manner whatsoever without written permission from the author, except in the case of brief quotations embodied in critical articles and reviews.

The Author of this book is solely responsible and liable for its content including but not limited to the views, representations, descriptions, statements, information, opinions and references ["Content"]. The Content of this book shall not constitute or be construed or deemed to reflect the opinion or expression of the Publisher or Editor. Neither the Publisher nor Editor endorse or approve the Content of this book or guarantee the reliability, accuracy or completeness of the Content published herein and do not make any representations or warranties of any kind, express or implied, including but not limited to the implied warranties of merchantability, fitness for a particular purpose. The Publisher and Editor shall not be liable whatsoever for any errors, omissions, whether such errors or omissions result from negligence, accident, or any other cause or claims for loss or damages of any kind, including without limitation, indirect or consequential loss or damage arising out of use, inability to use, or about the reliability, accuracy or sufficiency of the information contained in this book.

Made with ♥ on the Notion Press Platform
www.notionpress.com

*This book is dedicated to all students of BBA in Culinary Arts, MBA in Culinary Arts, B.Sc. HHA, MBATH and MSc Hotel Management. Your passion for the culinary and hospitality industries inspires the purpose of this book, which is to provide comprehensive knowledge and insights that empower your journey towards excellence in hospitality management and culinary arts.*

*With best wishes,*

### A NOTE FROM THE AUTHOR

*Dear Valuable Reader,*

*Thank you for purchasing his book. I will be grateful if you would send your details with Dr Sunil Kumar. Kindly click the link below or scan the QR Code to share your details and comments.*

*https://forms.gle/rLFVmnomwShwvmA6A*

**Scan QR Code to Submit Details**

# Contents

# Preface

"Food Quality Management: Textbook for UG & PG Students" is a comprehensive guide to food safety and excellence, designed for both undergraduate and professional students. The global food system is complex, and the demand for safe, nutritious, and high-quality food is increasing. This book provides a holistic understanding of the field, including core principles, cutting-edge techniques, and emerging trends.

The book begins by exploring the foundational pillars of quality management, emphasizing the importance of a clearly defined vision, mission, and unwavering customer focus. It then delves into food legislation, quality control methods, sensory evaluation, technology, globalization, food fraud, transparency, traceability, quality leadership, and practical application.

The text also addresses the challenges and opportunities presented by globalization, food fraud, and transparency in the global food market. It emphasizes the importance of strong quality management systems and stringent hygiene practices throughout the food chain. Engaging review questions reinforce knowledge and encourage critical thinking. By completing this book, students and professionals will gain a comprehensive understanding of the multifaceted world of food quality management, empowering them to contribute to the safety, integrity, and sustainability of the global food supply chain. This valuable reference guide will be readily available to support students and professionals in their career path. Students can also my blog visit

https://foodqulaitymanagement.blogspot.com/

Dr Sunil Kumar

Date: 09 Feb, 2025

# Acknowledgements

I extend my sincere gratitude to my supervisor, Professor (Dr.) Ashish Dahiya, whose unwavering patience and guidance were instrumental in the completion of this book. His support and encouragement provided the foundation for overcoming challenges and acquiring invaluable knowledge. Despite his busy schedule, he consistently offered valuable suggestions, and made corrections that significantly enhanced the quality of this work.

I am profoundly indebted to my family. Their unwavering support and understanding were indispensable throughout this journey.

Heartfelt appreciation goes to my friends who stood by me, offering strength and motivation. Your presence made a significant impact on the successful completion of this book.

I would also like to express my sincere gratitude to the MBA students in Tourism and Hospitality at Mizoram University. Your contributions through the PowerPoint presentations for this book have been invaluable. Your insights and perspectives have enriched the content, making it more comprehensive and applicable to a wider audience. Thank you for your dedication and collaboration in this project.

**Dr. Sunil Kumar**

CHAPTER I

# Quality Management Fundamentals

*""Excellence is a habit, and quality is the foundation of excellence.""*

`Quality standards vary from person to person due to their experience and knowledge about products and services. The Oxford American Dictionary defines quality as "**a degree or level of excellence**." This definition highlights that quality is inherently comparative, focusing on how one entity compares to another. However, quality is not just about comparison. It's also about meeting the needs and expectations of customers, whether those customers are consumers of products, users of services, or students in a classroom.

To quote Garvin, the idea of quality is very slippery; it's easy to picture but very hard to explain. When you hear the word "quality," you probably think of something general that is tough to quantify or pinpoint. When you say something is "quality," it makes sense. It refers to the standard that other groups like it are judged by and shows how great it is.

In the context of products or services, quality can be defined in several ways:

- **Conformance to Specifications:** How well a service or product meets the goals and limits set by the people who made it.
- **Fitness for Use:** How well the product performs its intended function or use.
- **Value for Price:** Whether or not the customer feels that the product provides value for its cost.
- **Support Services:** The quality of the after-sales service, customer support, and warranty claims.

**Concept of Quality: Historical Background**

The concept of quality as we think of it now first emerged from the Industrial Revolution. This led to the need for more formal quality control processes.

Quality management and quality assurance are terms that were first used in the second half of the 20th century. They have changed since then. For this amount of time, the quality industry has gone through more major changes than almost any other field. Quality management has changed over time. It used to focus on inspections to find problems. Now it uses statistical quality control to stop problems before they happen. Finally, it uses the all-encompassing approach of total quality management to get everyone in the organization involved in improving quality all the time.

Today, quality is seen as a strategic tool for competitiveness and success. Modern quality management encompasses lean manufacturing, which focuses on waste reduction; Six Sigma, a methodology for minimizing variation and defects; and continuous improvement through the application of Kaizen principles for ongoing enhancement. This involves establishing a pervasive culture of quality that influences all facets of the organization and brings benefits to various stakeholders, such as suppliers, employees, and customers.

## 1.1 Vision, Mission, and Quality Policy Statements

The strategic planning process of a business must include quality statements. They provide quality management initiatives focus, direction, and a guiding framework. Three essential components comprise quality statements:

### 1.1.1 Vision Statement

A vision statement represents an organization's desired future state, providing a clear direction and inspiring goal for its long-term aspirations. It is a source of inspiration and imagination, representing the ultimate goal that the organization aspires to achieve, typically over a long-term horizon of 5 to 10 years. A well-crafted vision statement not only serves as a brief guideline for decision-making but also aligns the efforts of leaders and employees towards a shared aspiration, fostering unity and direction.

Example: Disney Theme Park's vision statement, "The Happiest Place on Earth."

## 1.1.2 Mission Statement

A mission statement describes the organization's purpose, outlining the fundamental reason for its existence and guiding its strategic direction. It defines what the organization does and who it serves. A good mission statement answers the following questions:

- Who are we?
- Who are our customers?
- What do we do?
- How do we do it?

An effective mission statement offers a clear statement of purpose for employees, customers, and suppliers, encapsulating the organization's function concisely and in an easily understandable manner, fostering alignment and clarity among stakeholders.

Example: Ford Motor Company's mission statement: "To continually improve our products and services to meet our customers' needs, allowing us to prosper as a business and to provide a reasonable return to our shareholders, the owners of our business."

## 1.1.3 Quality Policy Statement

It is the job of everyone in the company to follow the quality policy statement when providing goods and services to customers. The approval of the quality board should be given after the CEO has heard what the employees have to say. A quality policy statement has to be part of an ISO 9000 quality management system. The paper sets the overall direction and goal for the business's quality management efforts. It makes it clear that the company is committed to meeting customer needs and improving processes all the time. Making sure that all employees follow the quality policy statement helps the company make sure that all of its goods and services are the same. This makes customers happier and more loyal. A company shows its dedication to quality management by putting in place and sticking to a quality policy statement. This also sets a standard for exceptional performance in both its goods and services.

Example: "Xerox is a quality company. Quality is the basic business principle for Xerox. Quality means providing our external and internal customers with innovative products and services that fully satisfy their requirements. Quality is the job of every employee."

## *1.2 Customer Focus*

Customer focus means consistently meeting and exceeding customer needs and standards. It shows that a company is dedicated to meeting and exceeding customer needs. Total Quality Management (TQM) is based on the idea that the people, not the company, should be the ones to decide how good a product or service is. Focusing on the customer means:

- Emphasis on customer-defined quality
- Emphasis on customer service
- Customer information is being used to create new products.
- Working with users to figure out new products, do research and development, and predict future technology

## 1.2.1 The Value of a Customer-Focused Approach

Customers are the most valuable asset of an organization, and their satisfaction is crucial to its success. As an indicator of quality, both manufacturing and service-oriented organizations employ consumer satisfaction. The key to achieving customer fulfillment is recognizing and fulfilling their expectations.

## 1.2.2 Implementing Customer Focus

To implement customer focus effectively, organizations should:

1. Conduct research to determine the requirements and expectations of customers.

2. Align the objectives of the organization with the requirements of its customers.

3. Engage in customer communication, assessment of satisfaction, and process improvement based on the findings.

4. Effectively manage relationships with customers.

5. Develop a strategy to reconcile the needs and desires of various stakeholders, including customers, employees, suppliers, investors, and proprietors.

## 1.2.3 Benefits of Being Customer-Focused

The advantages of prioritizing consumer needs and preferences include:

- Enhanced sales, revenue, market share, and mindshare.
- Robust consumer loyalty results in recurring patronage.
- Higher probability of content customers endorsing the products and services to others.

## 1.2.4 Customer Perception of Quality

Customer perception is how customers feel about a product, brand, or company. It is an opinion formed through every direct and indirect interaction with the organization. Understanding customer perception is crucial because it impacts every action customers take, influencing brand loyalty and the likelihood of generating referrals.

Four factors that influence customer perception are:

1. Customer reviews
2. Marketing efforts
3. Company values
4. Quality of customer support

## 1.2.5 Creating a Positive Customer Perception

To create a positive customer perception, organizations should:

1. Address and promptly take action based on consumer feedback.

2. Understand the target audience and their expectations.

3. Recognize and reward customer-centric behavior among employees.

4. Implement a customer-centric culture through active employee participation in consumer interactions.

## 1.3 Cost of Quality (COQ)

The Cost of Quality (CoQ) is a systematic approach utilized to quantify and define the resources that an organization devotes to preventive measures and the upkeep of service or product quality, in contrast to the expenses incurred due to internal and external malfunctions. It is the expense incurred as a result of substandard production.

This is the equation for cost-of-quality (CoQ):

CoQ = Cost of Good Quality (CoGQ) + Cost of Poor Quality (CoPQ)

## 1.3.1 Measuring the Cost of Quality

The cost of quality can be divided into four categories:

1. **Prevention Costs:** Costs incurred from activities intended to prevent failures (e.g., quality planning, employee training, quality improvement team meetings).

2. **Appraisal Costs:** Expenses invested in upholding satisfactory quality standards, such as audits of quality audits, process controls, and inspections of incoming materials.

3. **Internal Failure Expenses:** Expenses related to defects discovered prior to their delivery to the customer, such as refuse, rework, or waste resulting from inadequately designed processes.

4. **External Failure Costs:** Expenses related to service and repair, warranty claims, product returns, and other miscellaneous expenses incurred subsequent to the product's delivery to the consumer.

**Measuring the cost of quality is crucial for:**

- Early identification and resolution of quality issues
- conducting cost-benefit analyses on initiatives pertaining to process and quality improvement
- Evaluating quality performance in a single metric
- Identifying appropriate measures to address possible malfunctions

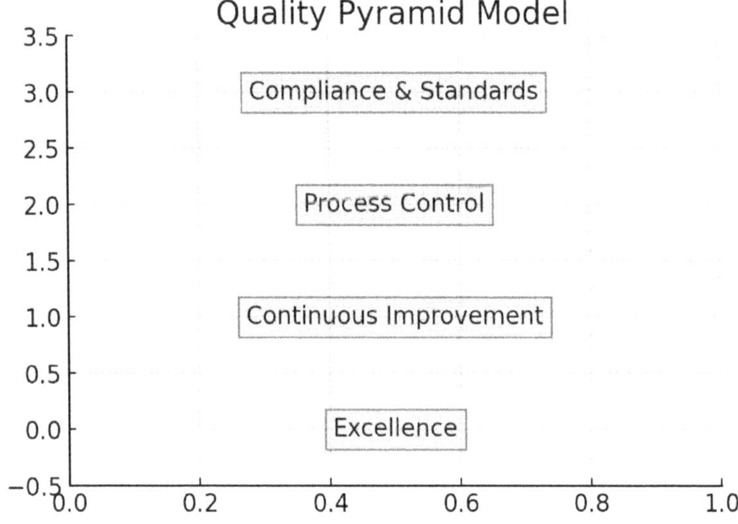

Quality Pyramid Modal

## *Review Questions*

1. Define a vision statement and provide an example.
2. What is the purpose of a mission statement?
3. Explain the importance of customer focus in quality management.
4. List the four factors that influence customer perceptions of quality.
5. What are the four categories of costs included in the cost of quality?
6. Discuss the three elements of quality statements (vision, mission, and quality policy) and their roles in an organization's strategic planning process.

7. Explain the benefits of being a customer-focused organization and suggest strategies for implementing customer focus effectively.

8. Describe the cost-quality equation and the significance of measuring the cost of quality in an organization.

**Short Questions**

(a) Mention at least four benefits of TQM.

b) Explain in detail the vision statement.

c) Define customer perception.

d) What do you mean by customer focus?

e) What is the importance of quality control?

f) How do I create an effective mission statement?

g) Define the Japanese 5S principles.

h) Differentiate between sort and set in order.

i) Define quality planning.

j) What do you understand by COQ (cost of quality)?

k) What is the significance of the customer in quality management?

l) Differentiate between vision and mission.

m) Mention at least four benefits of quality management.

n) Define quality.

o) Define TQM.

p) What do you mean by the cost of poor quality?

q) How are service standards defined?

r) How do you create an effective vision?

s) Define prevention costs.

t) Differentiate between internal failure and external failure.

u) Mention at least two TQM principles.

v) What do you mean by customer satisfaction?

w) What is the significance of vision and mission in an organization?

**Learning Activity:** Develop a vision, mission, and quality policy statement for a fictional organization of your choice. Discuss how these statements align with the organization's goals and values.

# CHAPTER II

# Contributions of Quality Pioneers

*"Innovation in quality is not about following the past but shaping the future."*

## 2.1 W. Edwards Deming and His 14 Points

Experienced as a statistician, W. Edwards Deming is considered a pioneer in the field of quality management. His contributions to Japanese industry during the 1950s were crucial in their ascent to the position of global leaders in terms of quality and productivity. The fourteen principles of Deming's theory furnish management with a comprehensive framework for enhancing quality, productivity, and competitive position.

**Deming's 14 Points:**

1. Foster an ongoing commitment to progress by prioritizing strategic foresight, discouraging immediate resolutions, and persistently endeavoring to implement more effective methodologies.

2. Implement the revised quality philosophy enterprise-wide, prioritizing customer requirements and embracing a substantial transformation in business procedures.

3. Cease relying on inspections, as they are impractical and expensive. Rather, incorporate quality into the entire process by employing statistical control methods.

4. To promote quality-driven partnerships and reduce variation, it is advisable to utilize a single supplier for each item, rather than focusing solely on price.

5. Emphasize training, education, and the Plan-Do-Check-Act methodology for process analysis and improvement while pursuing

perpetual and continuous improvement.

6. Implement on-the-job training to foster uniformity, establish a solid basis of shared knowledge, and promote efficient collaboration.

7. Establish leadership that provides guidance and support to personnel, empowering them to exceed their minimum obligations and achieve their maximum capabilities.

8. Cultivate an atmosphere devoid of apprehension, wherein employees are encouraged to openly communicate their thoughts and apprehensions, and where errors serve as chances for growth.

9. Foster interdepartmental collaboration, cross-functional cooperation, and a shared vision by dismantling barriers.

10. Prevent ambiguous slogans by establishing explicit expectations and commending exemplary performance in person, as opposed to depending on imprecise expressions.

11. Eliminate objective-based management, placing emphasis on the process rather than quantitative targets, while ensuring the provision of essential support and resources.

12. Eliminate obstacles to craftsmanship pride by ensuring equitable treatment for all employees and permitting them to exhibit pride in their work without assessment or comparison.

13. Establish educational and self-development initiatives to enhance existing proficiencies and equip oneself for forthcoming developments and obstacles.

14. Ensure that "transformation" is a collective responsibility, fostering an environment that promotes ongoing growth and recognition of the ways in which individual endeavors impact the overarching scheme of things.

## *2.2 Joseph M. Juran*

Joseph M. Juran, known for his exposure to Walter Shewhart's concepts at Western Electric, emphasized the necessity for management involvement in quality efforts. He introduced the Juran Trilogy, a framework for managing quality through three interrelated processes:

1. **Quality Planning:** Determine customer needs and develop processes and products to meet and exceed those needs, considering customer feedback and optimizing product features.

2. **Quality Control:** Ensure the process is running optimally, minimizing chronic waste, and implementing corrective actions when abnormal variations occur.

3. **Quality Improvement:** Continuously eliminate waste, defects, and rework to improve processes and reduce the cost of poor quality.

## 2.3 Armand V. Feigenbaum

An American quality expert named Armand V. Feigenbaum came up with the idea of total quality control (TQC), which was later used as the basis for total quality management (TQM). His most important achievements are:

1. **Total Quality Control:** An integrated system that focuses on quality development, maintenance, and improvement to provide cost-efficient manufacturing and service, resulting in increased customer satisfaction.

2. **Hidden Plant**: Feigenbaum asserted that 15% to 40% of an organization's capability is squandered due to first mistakes, highlighting the significance of dealing with this inefficiency known as the "hidden factory" of waste.

3. **Quality Accountability:** Quality is a universal concept, and every process and functional area is responsible and accountable for quality control within the organization.

4. **Quality Costs:** Feigenbaum established the concept of estimating the overall cost of quality, allowing company managers and quality specialists to assess actions based on cost reduction and profit increase.

## 2.4 Kaoru Ishikawa

Kaoru Ishikawa, known as the "Father of Japanese Quality," studied under Deming, Juran, and Feigenbaum. His major contributions include:

1. **Fishbone Diagram (Cause & Effect Diagram):** A tool for analyzing and identifying root causes of problems in industrial processes.

2. **Implementation of Quality Circles**: Volunteer groups of people who have been taught to find, analyze, and solve problems at work, which makes the organization better in many ways.

3. **Emphasis on Internal Customers:** Ishikawa advocated for overall participation from workers at all levels, recognizing the potential for quality contributions across the organization.

## *2.5 Philip B. Crosby*

Philip B. Crosby, author of "Quality is Free" and "Quality Without Tears," promoted the concept of "zero defects" and defined quality from the viewpoint of conformance to requirements. His approach focused on:

1. Four Absolutes of Quality:

1. Quality is defined as meeting specified specifications.
2. Quality system is based on prevention.
3. The performance standard is to achieve zero defects in relation to the criteria.
4. Quality is measured by the cost of not meeting the required standards.

2. "Do It Right the First Time": Focusing on meeting requirements from the outset rather than planning for and investing in strategies to address non-conformance.

3. Zero Defects and Zero Defects Day: Committing to defect-free products and services, with a designated day for management and employees to reaffirm their commitment to quality.

4. Crosby's Fourteen Steps: A systematic approach to quality improvement, including management commitment, quality measurement, corrective action, training, and continuous improvement.

## *2.6 Genichi Taguchi*

Genichi Taguchi, known for his contributions to quality control, developed:

1. **Loss Function:** A metric that combines cost, target, and variation into one measure, quantifying the relationship between customer experience and a company's profits.

2. **Signal-to-Noise Ratio:** A proactive equivalent to the loss function, used to identify and remove factors that affect the variability of a product.

3. **Orthogonal arrays:** cost-effective methods for isolating and removing indirect variables that influence product quality.

## *2.7 Japanese 5S Principles*

The 5S principles, originating from Japan, are a systematic approach to workplace organization and standardization, consisting of five steps:

1. Sort (Seiri): Identify and eliminate unnecessary items from the workplace.

2. Set in Order (Seiton): Arrange and designate essential items for effective retrieval and utilization.

3. Shine (Seiso): Ensure a tidy and orderly work environment by consistently cleaning and upkeeping it.

4. Standardize (Seiketsu): Create and record standards and procedures for sustaining the initial three steps.

5. Sustain (Shitsuke): Consistently oversee and maintain the established practices with discipline and dedication.

## *2.8 8D Methodology*

The 8D problem-solving technique is a structured, team-based way to fix important production problems. The goals are to find the root cause, come up with containment actions, and put corrective and preventative actions into place. These are the eight fields:

D0: Preparation (gathering information, resources, and expertise)

D1: Build a Problem-Solving Team

D2: Describe the problem (using the 5W2H approach).

D3: Temporarily Confine the Problem

D4: Analysis of the fundamental cause and identification of the point at which an issue or problem arises.

D5: Research and Develop Permanent Corrective Action

D6: Implement Permanent Corrective Actions

D7: Implement preventive actions.

D8: Appreciate Team Members and Document Learnings

## *2.9 Concepts of Quality Circles*

Quality circles are volunteer groups of workers who meet regularly to discuss and present ideas to management for improving various aspects of the workplace, such as product design, manufacturing processes, and organizational culture. They promote employee involvement, problem-solving, and continuous improvement.

## *Review Questions*

1. State Deming's 14th point: Make "transformation" everyone's job, encouraging continuous improvement and understanding how individual efforts contribute to the larger picture.

2. Define the Juran Trilogy: It is a framework for managing quality through three interrelated processes: quality planning, quality control, and quality improvement.

3. What is the "hidden plant" concept introduced by Feigenbaum? Feigenbaum stated that 15% to 40% of an organization's capacity is wasted by not getting things right the first time, emphasizing the importance of addressing this "hidden factory" of waste.

4. Name the tool developed by Ishikawa for root cause analysis: the fishbone diagram (cause and effect diagram).

5. Explain Crosby's concept of "zero defects": focusing on producing defect-free products and services to meet customer requirements without any deviations.

6. What is the purpose of Taguchi's loss function? It quantifies the relationship between customer experience and company profits by combining cost, target, and variation into one measure.

7. List the five steps of the Japanese 5S principles: sort (Seiri), set in order (Seiton), shine (Seiso), standardize (Seiketsu), and sustain (Shitsuke).

**Long Answer Questions:**

1. Discuss Deming's 14 points and their significance in improving quality, productivity, and competitive position.

2. Analyze Juran's approach to quality management, focusing on the quality planning, quality control, and quality improvement processes.

3. Explain Feigenbaum's contributions to Total Quality Control (TQC) and the importance of quality accountability within an organization.

4. Describe Ishikawa's emphasis on quality circles and the involvement of internal customers in quality management.

5. Evaluate Crosby's four absolutes of quality management and his systematic approach to quality improvement through his 14 steps.

6. Analyze Taguchi's loss function and signal-to-noise ratio and their roles in reducing product variability and improving the customer experience.

**Suggested Questions:**

1. What is the customer's perception of quality, and why is it important? Illustrate. Discuss the various factors that influence customer perception and how to create a positive customer perception of your company.

2. Compare the contributions of Ishikawa and Taguchi in quality. Explain in detail the contribution of each guru to quality control and process improvement.

3. Explain in detail the 8D methodology. Discuss each discipline.

4. Critically examine the contributions of quality gurus and discuss Deming's 14 points in detail.

5. Why is customer focus important for quality? Illustrate. Discuss the benefits and implementation of customer focus in an organization.

**Learning Activity:** Conduct a comparative analysis of the quality philosophies advocated by two quality pioneers. Identify similarities, differences, and their respective impacts on organizational performance.

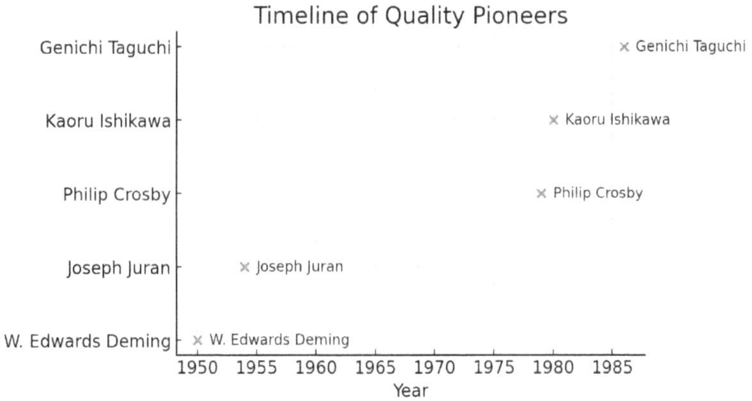


Timeline for Quality Pioneers

# CHAPTER III

# Introduction to Food Quality

*""True quality is not just about taste but trust—earned over time and through consistency.""*

## 3.1 Definition and Importance of Food Quality

The notion of food quality is comprehensive and encompasses various attributes of a food item that have an impact on its level of consumer acceptance. In addition to nutritional value, sensory attributes (such as flavor, texture, appearance, and aroma), and freshness and shelf life, it encompasses aspects beyond fundamental safety. Superior cuisine offers patrons a gratifying and secure dining encounter.

The importance of food quality can be understood from multiple perspectives:

- **Consumer Health and Safety:** Foodborne illnesses caused by contaminated or spoiled food can have serious health consequences. Maintaining quality helps prevent these illnesses. It ensures that the food is free from harmful bacteria, viruses, parasites, and chemical contaminants.
- **Consumer Satisfaction:** Consumers expect food to taste good, be nutritious, and meet their expectations. Consistent quality builds brand loyalty and trust. It also influences consumer perception and buying behavior.
- **Economic Benefits:** High-quality food reduces waste, recalls, and rework, leading to increased profitability for food businesses. It also opens up new market opportunities and can be a source of competitive advantage.

- **Market Reputation**: A commitment to quality enhances a company's reputation and competitiveness in the marketplace. It signals reliability and commitment to customer satisfaction.

## 3.2 Factors Affecting Food Quality

A complex interplay of intrinsic and extrinsic factors affects food quality.

**3.2.1 Intrinsic Factors**: These are the inherent properties of the food itself, determined during production and processing. They include:

- Raw material quality: The quality of the raw materials used in food production significantly influences the final product's quality. This includes the freshness of the ingredients, their origin, and the methods used to process them.
- Formulation: The ingredients used in a food product, their ratios, and the recipe used can all impact the quality of the final product.
- Processing methods: The techniques used to cook, preserve, and process the food can affect its quality. This includes cooking temperatures, cooking times, and the use of preservatives.
- Chemical composition: The nutrient content of the food, as well as the presence of natural toxins or contaminants, can affect its quality.
- Physical properties: The texture, color, and size of the food can all influence its perceived quality.

**3.2.2 Extrinsic Factors**: These are external factors that affect food quality after production. They include:

- Storage and handling conditions: The temperature and humidity at which food is stored can affect its shelf life and quality. Similarly, the way the food is handled during storage can also impact its quality.

- Transportation practices: The time taken to transport the food and the conditions under which it is transported can affect its quality.
- Preparation methods: The techniques used to prepare the food for consumption can influence its quality. This includes cooking techniques and portion control.
- Contamination risks: Environmental factors and cross-contamination during storage and preparation can affect food quality.
- Packaging integrity: The quality of the packaging material and any damage to the packaging can impact the quality of the food.

Understanding these factors is essential for implementing effective food quality management strategies.

## 3.3 Costs of Poor Quality in the Food Industry

Failing to maintain food quality can have significant financial repercussions for food businesses. These costs can be categorized as:

- **Prevention Costs:** These are the expenses associated with implementing quality control measures. This includes the cost of training staff on quality control procedures, conducting inspections, and testing products for quality.
- **Appraisal Costs:** These are the costs associated with monitoring and evaluating food quality. This includes the cost of sampling products for quality checks, conducting audits, and maintaining quality records.
- **Failure Costs:** These are the costs incurred due to poor quality products reaching the consumer. This includes the cost of recalls, rework, spoilage, and lawsuits. It also includes the cost of lost sales due to negative customer reviews and damage to the company's reputation.

In many cases, the cost of poor quality far exceeds the expenses incurred in prevention measures. Effective food quality management helps minimize failure costs and ensure a return on investment through preventive measures.

## *Importance of Food Quality*

**Consumer Perspective:**

Health and Safety: High-quality food ensures consumer health and safety by minimizing the risk of foodborne illnesses caused by contamination or spoilage. Consumers prioritize food products that meet stringent safety standards to protect themselves and their families.

Satisfaction and Experience: Quality food not only meets but exceeds consumer expectations regarding taste, freshness, nutritional value, and overall dining experience. Consumers derive satisfaction and enjoyment from consuming well-prepared, flavorful, and visually appealing food items.

**Industry Perspective:**

**Market Reputation:** Maintaining high food quality helps build a positive market reputation for food businesses. Consistently delivering superior-quality products earns consumer trust and loyalty, enhancing the company's brand image and fostering long-term relationships with customers.

**Competitiveness:** In today's competitive market landscape, offering high-quality food products gives businesses a competitive edge. Quality becomes a distinguishing factor that sets them apart from competitors, attracting discerning consumers who prioritize food quality over price.

**Profitability:** While ensuring food quality requires investment in resources and processes, it ultimately leads to increased profitability for businesses. Quality products command premium prices, reduce waste, minimize recalls and rework, and attract a larger customer base, resulting in improved financial performance and sustainable growth.

## *Review Questions:*

1. What are the key dimensions of food quality?
2. How can intrinsic factors like raw material quality influence food safety?
3. Explain the economic impact of food recalls due to poor quality.
4. Discuss the role of extrinsic factors in maintaining food quality.
5. How does the cost of poor quality affect the profitability of food businesses? Provide examples.

**Learning Activity:** Conduct a sensory evaluation of two food products with similar nutritional profiles but different quality attributes. Compare and contrast the sensory characteristics of each product, and discuss how they contribute to overall food quality.

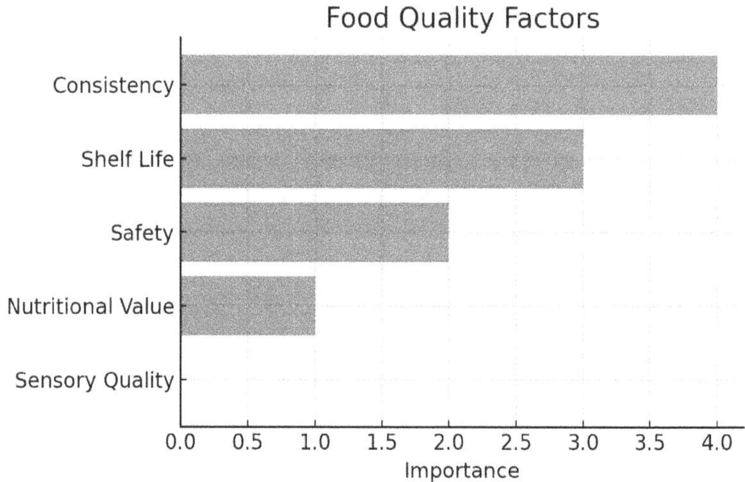


Food Quality Factors

# CHAPTER IV

# Food Quality Management Systems

*""What gets measured gets improved; what gets ignored gets compromised.""*

## 4.1 Concept of Food Quality Management Systems

Food Quality Management Systems (QMS) are systematic approaches implemented by stakeholders in the food industry to ensure the consistent provision of nutritious and secure food items to consumers. These systems comprise an assortment of policies, procedures, processes, and resources that are specifically engineered to oversee, regulate, and enhance the quality of food across the complete supply chain. They encompass an ongoing process of strategizing, executing, verifying, and enhancing the organization's activities in order to conform to the intended benchmarks of excellence.

## 4.2 Benefits of Implementing a Quality Management System

The implementation of a quality management system provides food industry stakeholders with numerous advantages:

- **Enhanced Food Safety:** By assisting in the identification and mitigation of potential hazards, QMS reduces the likelihood of foodborne illnesses and ensures regulatory compliance. It offers a methodical framework for the management of food safety hazards and the prevention of contamination.

- **Improved Product Quality:** By implementing quality control measures and standardized processes, QMS ensures consistency in product quality, leading to customer satisfaction and loyalty. It helps in maintaining the sensory attributes of the food, like taste, texture, color, and nutritional value.
- **Increased Efficiency:** Streamlined processes and improved resource management contribute to operational efficiency, reducing waste and costs. It helps in optimizing the use of resources, reducing rework, and improving productivity.
- **Regulatory Compliance:** Regulatory and industry standards adherence is facilitated by QMS frameworks such as Hazard Analysis and Critical Control Points (HACCP) and International Organization for Standardization (ISO) standards. It aids in the fulfillment of legal responsibilities and mitigates the likelihood of non-compliance.
- **Competitive Advantage:** Certification to recognized QMS standards enhances the reputation of food companies, demonstrating their commitment to quality and safety to consumers and stakeholders. It provides a competitive edge in the market and builds trust among consumers.

## *4.3 Different Quality Management Systems*

### *4.3.1 Hazard Analysis and Critical Control Points (HACCP)*

Using a structured approach, HACCP handles food safety well by finding, evaluating, and controlling possible risks that might happen at any point in the food production process. Fundamental HACCP principles include analyzing risks, finding key control points and limits, setting up monitoring systems and procedures, taking corrective actions, and keeping records. In the food business, HACCP certification is often needed to get into new markets and is widely accepted. It is a way of preventing problems that quickly and effectively keeps food safe.

## 4.3.2 ISO 22000

ISO 22000 is an international standard for systems that handle food safety. It was made by the International Organization for Standardization (ISO). By giving companies a structured way to handle food safety management, it protects the quality of food and builds customer trust. ISO 22000 lets companies show they care about food safety by getting certified. It does this by including the concepts of HACCP along with required programs and management system duties. No matter how big or complicated they are, every group in the food chain can use it.

## 4.3.3 Safe Quality Food (SQF)

To make sure that food is safe and of high quality, the Global Food Safety Initiative (GFSI) has approved Safe Quality Food (SQF). Its job is to keep an eye on food safety risks along the whole supply chain and make sure that products are of good quality. SQF certification covers all aspects of making sure food is safe and of good quality. It covers ideas of continuous improvement, quality management duties, and basic food safety rules. It sets strict rules for handling risks to food safety and making sure that businesses in the food industry can get safe goods.

## Review Questions:

1. Which elements comprise a product quality management system?
2. How does the implementation of a quality management system improve product quality and food safety?

3. In the culinary industry, what are the advantages of implementing a quality management system?
4. Specify the fundamental HACCP principles and its function in food safety management.
5. What is the shared importance of SQF and ISO 22000 in the management of food safety and quality? Illustrate with examples.
6. What are the ways in which a quality management system facilitates adherence to regulations and confers a competitive edge? Illustrate with examples.
7. Examine the function that continuous improvement serves within a quality management system. Illustrate with examples.
8. What role does a quality management system play in enhancing food industry efficiency? Illustrate with examples.
9. Standardized processes' function within a quality management system is to be discussed. Illustrate with examples.
10. What is the role of a quality management system in fostering consumer confidence? Illustrate with examples.
11. Certification's function within a quality management system is to be examined. Illustrate with examples.

**Learning Activity:** Develop a quality management plan for a hypothetical food manufacturing company. Outline the key components of the plan, including quality objectives, process controls, and monitoring procedures, based on a chosen QMS framework.

PDCA Cycle for Quality Management
Act
Check
Do
Plan
Plan
Do
Check
Act
0.0   0.5   1.0   1.5   2.0   2.5   3.0   3.5   4.0

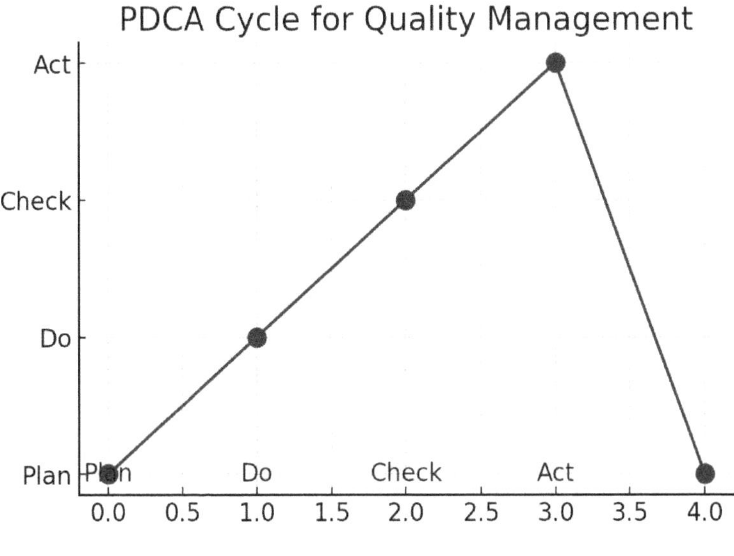

PDCA

# Food Legislation and Regulatory Requirements

*""Laws protect the consumer, but ethical responsibility safeguards the future."*

It talks about how Codex Alimentarius sets global standards and how national regulatory bodies like the FSSAI (India) and FDA (USA) make sure that food is safe for consumers.

## 5.1 International Food Standards (Codex Alimentarius)

**Structure and Function:**

- Codex Alimentarius Commission (CAC): The CAC was established as an intergovernmental organization by the FAO and WHO. It is composed of expert committees and member nations that collaborate to establish agricultural standards. The purpose of these scientifically supported standards is to safeguard consumer health and promote equitable practices within the food industry.
- The development of Codex standards follows a meticulous process that includes risk assessment, the proposal of draft standards, review by scientific experts, and adoption by member countries. It begins with a risk assessment to identify potential food safety issues. The next step is for scientific experts to propose and evaluate draft standards. Finally, member nations adopt the standards and incorporate them into their national legislation.

- Codex standards offer significant benefits by facilitating international trade through harmonization, ensuring consumer protection by setting food safety requirements, and promoting fair practices in the global food trade.
- Facilitate international trade: Codex standards provide a reference point for countries when developing their national food safety regulations. This harmonization of standards helps to facilitate international food trade by reducing technical barriers.
- Consumer protection: Codex standards contribute to ensuring safe food for consumers globally. They set out requirements for food hygiene, additives, residues of veterinary drugs, and more.
- Fair practices: Codex standards help to prevent unfair competition in the international food trade. They ensure that all countries have access to the same food safety and quality requirements, regardless of their level of development.

**Challenges and Limitations:**

- The meticulous scientific review process and the need for consensus among member countries often lead to delays in the development and implementation of Codex standards. This is due to the need for scientific review and consensus-building among member countries.
- Balancing diverse national perspectives on acceptable risk levels and dietary habits poses challenges in aligning Codex standards with the specific food safety priorities of individual countries. For example, countries may have different views on acceptable levels of risk or different dietary habits that need to be considered.

# 5.2 National Regulatory Bodies and Legislations

- **Comparison of Regulatory Frameworks:** Various nations have established distinct regulatory frameworks pertaining to food protection. As an illustration, a comprehensive set of food safety regulations governs all phases of the food chain in the European Union. In contrast, the regulatory system in Brazil is more fragmented, with various agencies tasked with overseeing distinct facets of food safety.
- **Focus on Specific Regulations:** National regulatory bodies enforce a range of specific food safety regulations. These may include regulations on food labeling (such as nutritional information, allergen declarations, and origin labeling), maximum residue limits for pesticides, and microbiological standards for specific food categories (e.g., milk, meat).
- **Enforcement Mechanisms:** National regulatory bodies ensure compliance with food safety regulations through mechanisms such as licensing procedures, regular inspections, sampling programs, and penalties for non-compliance. These may include licensing and registration procedures for food businesses, regular inspections of food facilities, sampling and testing programs, and penalties for non-compliance with regulations. In cases of safety concerns, food recall procedures may be initiated.

## *5.3 Emerging Trends in Food Safety Regulation*

A growing focus on traceability, regulatory considerations for new food technologies (e.g., genetically modified organisms), and challenges and rules linked to online food sales are some new trends in food safety regulation. Traceability systems make it possible to keep track of food products all the way through the supply chain. This makes it safer and easier to respond faster to cases of foodborne diseases. New food technologies make it harder to regulate food safety because they need risk assessments and safety assessments. As online food sales have grown, it has become harder to keep food safe while it is being delivered and stored.

## *5.4 Enforcement and Compliance Mechanisms*

Regulatory authorities play a crucial role in ensuring food safety and quality standards throughout the food supply chain. They employ various enforcement mechanisms, including inspection protocols, sampling and testing procedures, surveillance systems, regulatory audits, penalties for non-compliance, and corrective actions and remediation. Inspection protocols assess compliance with food safety regulations, hygiene practices, and quality standards. Sampling and testing procedures collect samples of food products, ingredients, and environmental surfaces for laboratory analysis. Surveillance systems monitor trends in foodborne illnesses and contamination incidents, while regulatory audits evaluate the effectiveness of food safety management systems. Penalties for non-compliance may include fines, product recalls, license suspension, and legal action. Regulatory authorities continually adapt their approaches to address evolving food safety challenges and ensure the highest standards of food quality and integrity.

## *Review Questions:*

1. What is the role of the Codex Alimentarius Commission in setting global food standards?
2. How do Codex standards facilitate international food trade?
3. What are some of the challenges in developing and implementing Codex standards?
4. How do national regulatory bodies enforce food safety regulations?
5. What are some specific food safety regulations enforced by national regulatory bodies?
6. What are some emerging trends in food safety regulation?
7. How does traceability enhance food safety?

8. What are some regulatory considerations for novel food technologies?
9. How do online food sales pose challenges for food safety regulation?
10. What resources are available for further exploration of food legislation and regulatory requirements?

**Learning Activity:** Conduct a regulatory compliance audit for a food business operating in a specific country. Identify relevant regulations, assess the business's compliance status, and recommend corrective actions to address any non-compliance issues.

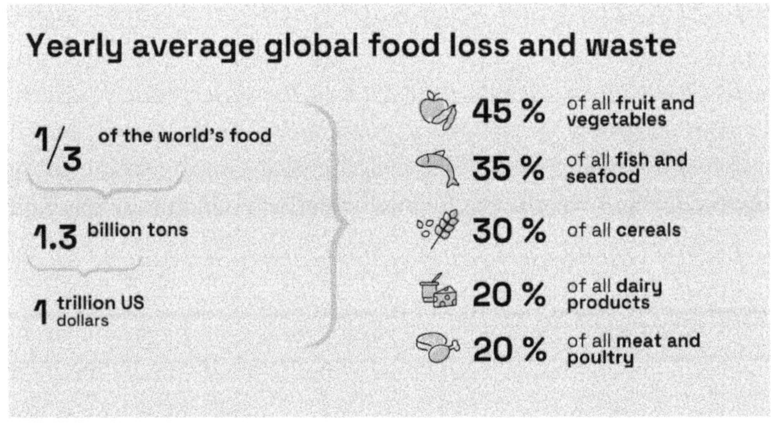


Global Food Loss and Waste

# CHAPTER VI

# Principles of Quality Control

*""Quality is not what you put into a product; it's what the customer gets out of it."*

A vital component of the culinary industry, quality control ensures that products meet predetermined criteria for safety, consistency, and quality. This chapter provides an in-depth analysis of the fundamentals of quality control, with an emphasis on sampling methods, statistical process control techniques, and the significance of calibration and validation.

## 6.1 Statistical Process Control (SPC) Techniques

Statistical Process Control (SPC) is a quality control technique that oversees and manages a process by utilizing statistical methodologies. This guarantees that the process runs efficiently, leading to a decrease in waste and an increased production of items meeting the criteria. Statistical Process Control (SPC) can be used for any process that allows for the measurement of products that meet the given criteria.

- **Control Charts:** Control charts, commonly referred to as Shewhart charts or process-behavior charts, are statistical tools used to assess whether a manufacturing or business process is operating within acceptable limits.
- **Common Types of Control Charts:**

  - X-bar chart is utilized to track the process mean and detect any shifts in the process average.

- R chart is utilized to observe the dispersion or variability of a process to determine its consistency over time.
- c-chart: Utilized for monitoring the defect count per unit.
- U chart is utilized to monitor the quantity of failures per unit in a process.

- **Benefits of SPC:**

  - It enables proactive identification and prevention of quality issues, reducing the occurrence of defects and rework.
  - Supports ongoing process improvement initiatives by offering data-based insights on process efficiency.

## 6.2 Sampling Techniques for Food Quality Evaluation

Sampling is a critical component of food quality control. It involves selecting a subset of products from a larger batch to evaluate their quality characteristics. The results are then generalized to the entire batch.

- **Sampling plan:** A sampling plan is a detailed sequence of sample selections, each of which may correspond to different locations, times, or conditions.
- **Sampling methods:**

  - Random sampling: Each unit in the lot has an equal chance of being selected, ensuring a representative sample.
  - Stratified sampling: The lot is divided into sub-groups (strata) based on a specific characteristic, and samples are drawn from each stratum.
  - Systematic sampling: Samples are selected at regular intervals throughout the lot.

- **Sample size:** the number of units selected for testing, determined based on the desired level of confidence and the expected variability in the lot.
- **Sample handling and storage:** Proper procedures for handling and storing samples are crucial to prevent contamination or deterioration before analysis.

## 6.3 Importance of Calibration and Validation in Quality Control

Calibration and validation are essential components of a robust quality control system. They ensure that instruments and methods used in quality control produce accurate and reliable results.

- **Calibration:** Calibration is the act of adjusting an instrument to get a measurement for a sample that falls within an acceptable range. The process entails comparing the measurements of two distinct systems: one with established uncertainties (standards) and another utilized for measuring the same parameter.
- **Validation:** Validation is the process of evaluating a system during the design and development of the system to meet the system requirements: concept, design, fabrication, final inspection, packing, shipping, and post-delivery.

## Review Questions:

1. What is the purpose of statistical process control (SPC) in quality control?
2. Describe the different types of control charts used in the SPC.
3. What are the benefits of using SPC in quality control?
4. Explain the different sampling techniques used for food quality evaluation.

5. Why is it important to determine the sample size in food quality evaluation?
6. What is the importance of sample handling and storage in food quality evaluation?
7. Explain the process of calibration in quality control.
8. What is the purpose of validation in quality control?
9. How do quality control principles contribute to food safety and consistency?
10. Why is quality control important in the food industry?

**Learning Activity:** Design an SPC chart for monitoring the temperature of a food processing operation. Collect temperature data over a specified time period, plot the data on the SPC chart, and analyze the results to identify any out-of-control conditions and potential sources of variation.

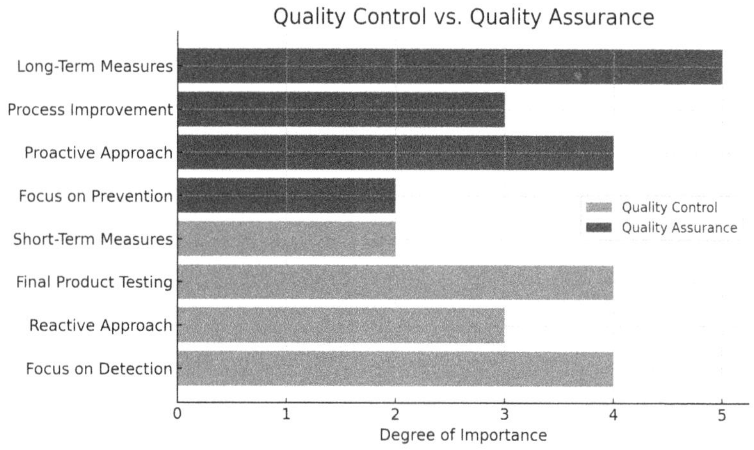


Quality Control Vs Quality Assurance

# CHAPTER VII

# Food Quality Assurance Programs

*""Assurance is not just about compliance; it's about confidence in every bite."*

In today's global food industry, ensuring food safety and quality across the production chain is essential. Prerequisite Programs (PRPs), Hazard Analysis and Critical Control Points (HACCP), and Preventive Controls and Food Safety Plans (FSVP) are three essential programs that are essential to guaranteeing food quality and are covered in this chapter. By understanding and putting these techniques into practice, food companies may lower the risk of foodborne illness, boost consumer confidence, and ensure consistent product quality.

## *7.1 Hazard Analysis and Critical Control Points (HACCP) Principles*

HACCP is a methodical and science-driven strategy for managing food safety. It identifies, prevents, and controls biological, chemical, and physical dangers from raw materials to completed products in a proactive manner. HACCP, developed by Codex Alimentarius, is globally acknowledged as a fundamental aspect of food safety.

**The Seven HACCP Principles:**

HACCP follows a logical sequence of seven principles that guide the development and implementation of a robust food safety plan:

**Conduct a Hazard Analysis:** At the outset, it is important to identify all potential dangers linked to every stage of food production. Take into account biological threats such as germs and viruses, chemical hazards like pesticides and cleaning agents, and physical hazards such as glass shards and metal particles that may contaminate the food product. **Example:** During a hazard analysis for raw chicken processing, potential hazards might include Salmonella bacteria (biological), residual chlorine from sanitation (chemical), and bone fragments (physical).

**Identify Critical Control Points (CCPs):** A CCP is a specific point in the manufacturing process where measures can be implemented to prevent, eliminate, or decrease recognized hazards to safe levels. Identifying Critical Control Points (CCPs) involves a thorough evaluation of the food product, processing procedures, and potential risks. **Example:** In chicken processing, CCPs could include cooking temperature to eliminate Salmonella, chlorine concentration in the washing stage, and metal detection to identify bone fragments.

**Establish Critical Limits for Each CCP:** For each CCP, define specific parameters (e.g., temperature, time, pH) that must be maintained to ensure food safety. These critical limits are science-based and derived from regulations, research, or industry best practices. **Example:** The critical limit for cooking chicken to eliminate Salmonella might be an internal temperature of 165°F (74°C) for a specific cooking time.

**Establish Monitoring Procedures:** Consistent surveillance of Critical Control Points (CCPs) is essential to verify that essential thresholds are being maintained. Monitoring techniques can vary from basic temperature assessments to intricate laboratory examinations, depending on the Critical Control Point (CCP) and the specific threat.

**Example:** Cooking temperatures in chicken processing could be monitored using digital thermometers with alarms, while chlorine concentrations in wash water might be monitored with test strips.

**Establish Corrective Actions:** A plan for corrective actions must be developed for each CCP. These actions should be implemented immediately if monitoring reveals a deviation from the critical limit. Corrective actions may involve adjusting processing parameters, rejecting contaminated products, or conducting further testing. **Example:** If chicken fails to reach the critical cooking temperature, corrective actions could involve extending cooking time, reprocessing the batch, or discarding the contaminated product.

**Establish Verification Procedures:** Verification procedures confirm the effectiveness of the entire HACCP system. This can involve internal audits, reviewing monitoring records, and periodically testing finished products for potential hazards. **Example:** Regular audits of the HACCP plan by a qualified food safety professional could be used for verification.

**Maintain Documentation:** It is crucial to keep thorough and accurate records of all HACCP operations. The hazard analysis, CCP identification, critical limits, monitoring data, remedial actions implemented, and verification activities are all included in this documentation. These documents support the ongoing development of the HACCP system and show a dedication to food safety.

**Benefits of HACCP:**

- **Proactive Approach:** Prevents hazards rather than reacting to outbreaks.
- **Science-Based System:** Uses scientific principles for hazard identification and control.
- **Versatility:** applicable to diverse food products and processing operations.
- **Internationally Recognized:** Provides a framework for global food safety standards.

**Limitations of HACCP:**

- **Resource Intensive:** Implementing and maintaining HACCP requires dedicated personnel and expertise.
- **Focus on CCPs:** Hazards outside identified CCPs may require additional control measures.
- **Continuous Monitoring:** Effective HACCP necessitates ongoing monitoring and record-keeping.

## *7.2 Pre-Requisite Programs (PRPs)*

PRPs are essential hygiene and sanitation programs that create the fundamental conditions required for the successful execution of HACCP. They establish a foundational framework for food safety through addressing basic hygiene standards, facility cleanliness, and maintenance processes.. Examples of PRPs: Good Manufacturing Practices (GMPs):

**Good Manufacturing Practices (GMPs):**

GMPs are recommendations that establish the minimal requirements for maintaining clean facilities, equipment, and people procedures to prevent contamination during food processing. They cover a broad spectrum of elements, such as:

- **Facility Design and Construction:** Ensuring proper building design and materials to facilitate cleaning and prevent pest harborage.
- **Equipment Maintenance:** Implementing procedures for cleaning, sanitizing, and maintaining equipment to prevent contamination of food products.
- **Personnel Hygiene:** training employees on proper hygiene practices, including handwashing and proper attire, and preventing contamination from personnel.
- **Pest Control:** Establishing procedures for preventing and managing pest infestations within food production facilities.
- **Waste Management:** Implementing a plan for safe and sanitary disposal of food waste and other waste materials.
- **Sanitation Standard Operating Procedures (SSOPs):** Developing and implementing specific procedures for cleaning and disinfecting food contact surfaces, equipment, and facilities. SSOPs ensure consistent and effective sanitation practices throughout the production process.
- **Supplier Quality Assurance Programs:** Evaluating and approving suppliers to ensure the safety and quality of incoming

raw materials and ingredients.

**Importance of PRPs:**

- **Foundation for HACCP:** Well-implemented PRPs are crucial for the successful establishment and upkeep of a HACCP system. PRPs reduce the risk of contamination in the food production chain by focusing on fundamental hygiene and sanitation procedures.
- **Preventative Measures:** PRPs focus on **preventing** contamination by establishing good hygiene practices and sanitation procedures. This proactive approach reduces the reliance on end-product testing and contributes to a more consistent level of food safety.
- **Consumer Protection:** By establishing a clean and hygienic environment for food production, PRPs play a vital role in protecting consumers from foodborne illness.

**Example: Implementing PRPs in a Bakery**
A bakery implementing PRPs might include:

- Ensuring a hygienic facility with smooth, non-absorbent surfaces that are easy to clean and disinfcct.
- Consistently cleaning and sanitizing all surfaces, equipment, and utensils that come into touch with food.
- Providing instruction to employees on correct handwashing procedures and food safety protocols.
- Establishing a pest management strategy to deter rodent and insect infestations.
- Developing protocols for the secure storage and proper management of unprocessed materials and final goods.
- Creating Standard Sanitation Operating Procedures (SSOPs) for cleaning and sanitizing designated locations and equipment utilized in the bakery.

By implementing these PRPs, the bakery creates a foundation for safe food production and lays the groundwork for a successful HACCP system.

## 7.3 Preventive Controls and Food Safety Plans (FSVP) for Importers

The FSVP rule, enforced by the US Food and Drug Administration (FDA), aims to prevent food hazards in imports to the United States. Foreign food facilities producing food for export to the USA must create and execute a Food Safety Plan (FSVP).

**FSVP vs. HACCP: Similarities and Differences**

The FSVP framework shares some similarities with HACCP principles but emphasizes specific aspects of food safety for imported foods:

- **Hazard Analysis:** FSVP targets potential risks that are likely to happen and could result in severe negative health effects or death in humans. This approach is more focused than the comprehensive hazard analysis in HACVP.
- **Preventive Controls:** FSVP emphasizes establishing and implementing preventive measures to control identified hazards throughout the supply chain, from the foreign supplier to the US importer.
- **Verification:** FSVP requires ongoing monitoring, verification, and corrective action procedures to ensure the effectiveness of the FSVP plan. Similar to HACCP, verification activities confirm that the preventive controls are working as intended.

**Importance of FSVP:**

- **Enhanced Food Safety:** Prevents hazards in imported food products, protecting US consumers from foodborne illness associated with imported foods.

- **Risk-Based Approach:** Focuses on hazards with the greatest potential for harm, prioritizing resources for the most critical controls.
- **Harmonization** aligns with internationally recognized food safety principles like HACCP, facilitating the global trade of safe food products.

**Example: FSVP for a Spice Importer**

A company importing spices from India would need to develop an FSVP plan that addresses potential hazards associated with spices, such as microbial contamination (e.g., Salmonella) or mycotoxins (produced by mold). The FSVP plan might involve:

- Performing a hazard analysis to detect potential dangers.
- Evaluating the risks linked to the listed hazards.
- Implementing preventive measures with the Indian spice supplier, such as adopting good agricultural practices (GAP) or good manufacturing practices (GMPs),

## *Review Questions:*

1. What is the role of effective leadership in establishing and upholding a culture of quality within food management systems?
2. How do leaders convert the overarching vision of the organization into quantifiable, transparent quality goals?
3. Discuss the key strategies for fostering motivation among employees in the food management sector.
4. How does setting clear and achievable goals for individuals and teams contribute to a quality-driven workforce?
5. What are the benefits of fostering a collaborative environment and promoting diversity within teams in achieving quality objectives?

6. How does recognizing and rewarding employee contributions reinforce a culture of quality and motivate continued engagement?
7. Discuss the benefits of fostering employee involvement in quality initiatives.
8. How does employee involvement lead to enhanced problem-solving and innovation in food management systems?
9. How can engaged employees contribute to increased productivity and efficiency in food management systems?
10. How does employee involvement in quality initiatives lead to a stronger customer focus within the organization?

**Learning Activity:** Develop a HACCP plan for a specific food product manufacturing process. Identify potential hazards, establish critical control points, determine control measures, and develop monitoring, verification, and corrective action procedures based on HACCP principles.

HACCP Flowchart
Documentation
Verification
Corrective Actions
Monitor
Set Limits
Determine CCPs
Identify Hazards
0.96    0.98    1.00    1.02    1.04

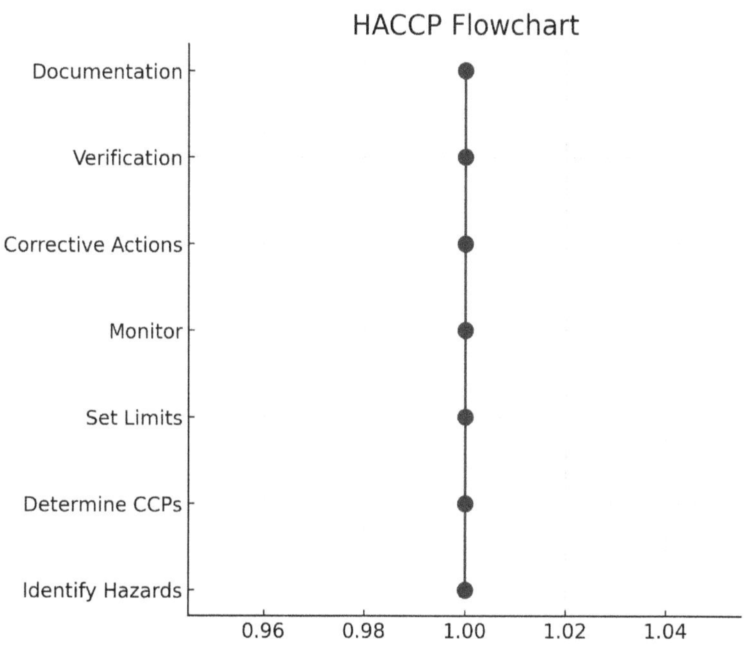

HACCP

# CHAPTER VIII

# Sensory Evaluation of Food Quality

*"*"The true test of quality is not in the label but in the experience of the senses."*"*

## 8.1 Sensory Analysis Techniques: Decoding the Senses

Sensory analysis is a scientific discipline that utilizes human senses, including taste, smell, sight, touch, and hearing, to evaluate food quality. It involves two main techniques:

## 8.1.1 Descriptive Sensory Analysis: Painting a Detailed Sensory Picture

Descriptive sensory analysis focuses on the objective description and quantification of a product's sensory attributes. Imagine a team of trained panelists meticulously evaluating a new chocolate bar. Using a standardized vocabulary and scaling methods, they might describe the appearance (color, glossiness), texture (snap, melt-in-your-mouth feel), aroma (cocoa intensity, fruity notes), taste (sweetness level, bitterness), and even the sound (initial snap, lingering smoothness).

This detailed sensory profiling provides crucial information for:

**Product Development:** By pinpointing specific sensory characteristics, descriptive analysis enables developers to enhance product quality, streamline production processes, identify areas for improvement, and ensure consistency between batches.

**Quality Control:** Monitoring sensory profiles over time helps identify deviations from established standards, enabling corrective actions to maintain product quality.

**Sensory Comparisons:** Descriptive analysis facilitates objective comparisons between different samples, whether it's comparing a new recipe iteration to the original or evaluating competitor products.

## 8.1.2 Affective Sensory Analysis: Decoding Consumer Preferences

While descriptive analysis focuses on the "what" of sensory perception, affective sensory analysis delves into the "how" and "why" of consumer preferences. This technique aims to understand consumer liking, disliking, and acceptance of food products. Common methods include:

Hedonic Testing: Panelists rate their overall liking or disliking of a product on a labeled scale (e.g., dislike extremely, like extremely).

Acceptance Testing: Consumers evaluate their willingness to purchase or consume a product (e.g., would definitely buy or would definitely not buy).

**Affective sensory analysis provides invaluable insights for:**

Market Research: Understanding consumer preferences helps manufacturers tailor products to meet market demands and maximize customer satisfaction.

New Product Launch Success: By gauging consumer acceptance through affective testing, manufacturers can predict a product's potential success in the marketplace and refine formulations accordingly.

Product Differentiation: Sensory analysis helps identify unique sensory attributes that distinguish products from competitors, aiding in effective marketing strategies.

## 8.2 Training and Selection of Sensory Panelists

The selection and training of sensory panelists are paramount to obtaining reliable and consistent sensory evaluations. Ideal panelists possess the following characteristics:

- Keen Sensory Acuity: Panelists should have well-developed sensory abilities, particularly in taste and smell.
- Discrimination Ability: The ability to distinguish subtle differences between sensory attributes is crucial for accurate evaluations.
- Articulation Skills: Panelists must effectively communicate their sensory perceptions using precise terminology.
- Objectivity: Evaluations should be based solely on sensory observations, free from personal biases or preferences.

**Training Programs:**
Once selected, panelists undergo rigorous training programs that typically involve:

- Sensory Attribute Familiarization: Panelists learn to identify and differentiate between various sensory characteristics of specific food products.
- Standardization of Evaluation Procedures: Training ensures consistent evaluation methods across panelists, including proper sample handling, tasting techniques, and data recording.
- Calibration of Sensory Responses: Panelists participate in calibration exercises to ensure their sensory perceptions are aligned and reliable.

Maintaining Panelist Performance:
Regular monitoring and refresher training sessions are essential to maintain panelist performance, uphold the reliability of sensory evaluations over time, and ensure the continued accuracy and consistency of sensory assessments.

## 8.3 *Applications of Sensory Evaluation in Food Quality Control*

Sensory evaluation is a versatile tool that plays a vital role in ensuring food quality control across various stages of the production process. Here are some key applications:

**New Product Development**: Sensory analysis helps assess the acceptability and appeal of new product concepts, allowing for refinement and optimization before market launch.

**Monitoring Product Consistency:** Regular sensory evaluation ensures batch-to-batch consistency by identifying any deviations from established sensory profiles. Early detection of these variations allows for corrective actions to maintain product quality.

**Understanding Consumer Preferences:** Affective sensory analysis provides valuable insights into consumer likings and dislikes.

**Evaluating Shelf Life and Stability:** Sensory analysis plays a crucial role in assessing how a product's sensory attributes change over time under different storage conditions. This information is vital for determining product shelf-life and identifying optimal storage conditions to maintain sensory quality throughout its intended lifespan. For example, sensory evaluation can be used to track how a cookie's texture changes (becomes softer or crumblier) or how the aroma and flavor of a yogurt might change during storage.

**Troubleshooting Quality Issues**: When unexpected quality issues arise, sensory evaluation can be a valuable tool for pinpointing the source of the problem. For instance, if consumers complain about an off-flavor in a new batch of potato chips, sensory analysis can help identify if the issue lies with a change in the type of oil used for frying, a fluctuation in spice levels, or even a storage issue that has impacted the flavor profile.

By incorporating sensory evaluation into a comprehensive food quality control program, manufacturers gain a deeper understanding of their products' sensory characteristics and consumer preferences. This knowledge empowers them to:

Ensure Consistent Production of High-Quality Products: By monitoring sensory profiles and identifying deviations, manufacturers can maintain consistent quality and minimize the risk of defective products reaching consumers.

**Meet Consumer Expectations:** Understanding consumer preferences through affective testing allows manufacturers to develop and refine products that cater to market demands and maximize customer satisfaction.

**Gain a Competitive Advantage:** Sensory analysis can help identify unique sensory attributes that differentiate a product from competitors, informing marketing strategies and product positioning.

Sensory evaluation is not merely about taste testing; it's a scientific discipline that provides a powerful tool for ensuring food quality control throughout the production chain. By strategically leveraging the human senses and employing rigorous methodologies, sensory analysis offers valuable insights that are essential for the development, optimization, and overall success of food products in today's competitive market.

## *Review Questions*

1. What is the difference between descriptive and affective sensory analysis?
2. Why is the selection and training of sensory panelists important?
3. How can sensory evaluation be applied to food quality control?
4. What are some of the sensory attributes that can be evaluated in a food product?
5. How does affective sensory analysis help in understanding consumer preferences?
6. What role does sensory evaluation play in new product development?
7. Why is consistency important in sensory evaluation?
8. How can sensory evaluation techniques be used to improve food quality?

9. What factors should be considered when selecting sensory panelists?
10. How does sensory evaluation contribute to the success of a food product on the market?

**Learning Activity:** Conduct a sensory evaluation study to assess the sensory attributes of a food product. Recruit and train sensory panelists, design sensory tests, collect and analyze sensory data, and interpret the results to make informed decisions about product quality and improvement opportunities.

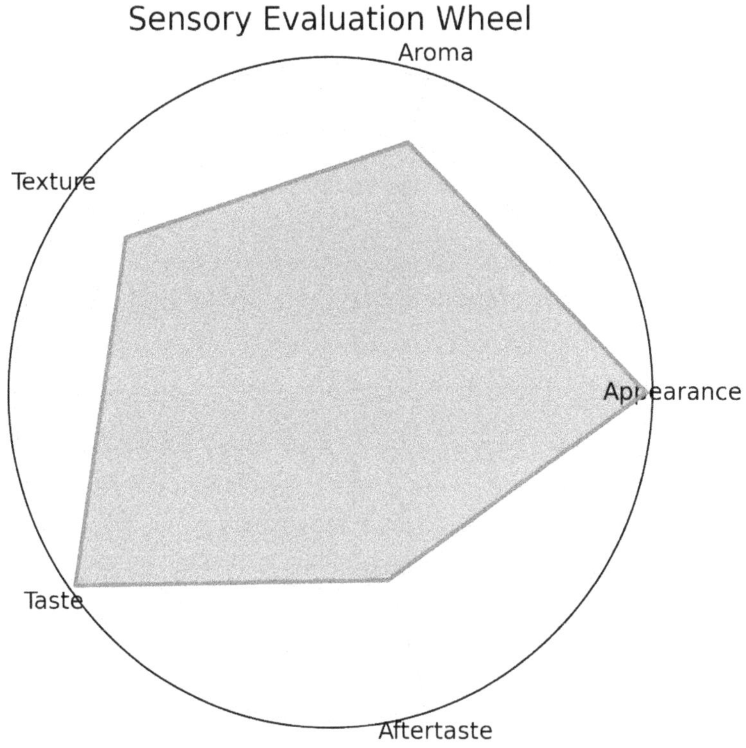


Sensory Evaluation Wheel

# CHAPTER IX

# Quality Management in Primary Production (Agriculture)

*""A nation's health depends on the quality of its soil, seeds, and stewardship.""*

Quality management in primary production, particularly in agriculture, forms the cornerstone of a safe, reliable, and sustainable food system. This chapter delves into the essential aspects of quality management practices in primary production, encompassing Good Agricultural Practices (GAP), pre-harvest handling and storage techniques, and the critical role of traceability in the food chain.

## 9.1 Good Agricultural Practices (GAP): A Holistic Approach

Good Agricultural Practices (GAP) are a collection of ideas and guidelines designed to encourage safe and responsible agricultural production. GAP includes food safety, economic viability, social responsibility, and environmental sustainability. Farmers can use GAP to maintain the quality and integrity of their goods, reduce environmental impact, and support a sustainable food system.

**Soil and Water Management**: Sustainable practices for maintaining **soil fertility** through nutrient management, cover cropping, and crop rotation. These practices help prevent **soil erosion** and ensure the long-term health and productivity of agricultural land. Water resources are managed efficiently through practices like irrigation scheduling and precision agriculture techniques to conserve water and minimize waste.

**Crop Management:** GAP emphasizes **informed crop selection** based on factors like climate, soil type, and market demand. Planting practices focus on using high-quality seeds and seedlings, while cultivation techniques promote healthy plant growth and minimize the need for chemical inputs. **Integrated Pest Management (IPM)** strategies are encouraged, which combine biological, cultural, and mechanical methods to control pests and diseases while minimizing reliance on chemical pesticides.

**Harvesting and Post-Harvest Handling:** GAP provides guidelines for harvesting crops at the ideal stage of maturity to guarantee maximum quality, flavor, and nutritional content. Effective handling techniques reduce harm during harvesting and transit by utilizing suitable containers and ensuring sufficient temperature control. Post-harvest storage facilities need to be constructed to preserve freshness and quality by regulating temperature, humidity, and ventilation.

**Worker Health and Safety:** GAP prioritizes establishing a secure and conducive work environment for agricultural laborers. This involves offering instruction on safe handling procedures, the utilization of personal protective equipment (PPE), and cleanliness routines to avoid occupational risks.

**Environmental Conservation:** Sustainable land management practices are encouraged to minimize environmental impacts. GAP promotes strategies like reducing chemical inputs, promoting biodiversity through habitat creation, and implementing soil conservation techniques to protect natural resources for future generations.

**Examples of GAP implementation:**

**Fruit and Vegetable Production:** Crop rotation helps break disease cycles and maintain soil health. Cover cropping improves soil fertility and reduces erosion. Biological pest control methods like introducing beneficial insects can minimize reliance on chemical pesticides.

**Livestock Production:** Providing animals with clean water, proper nutrition, and adequate space promotes animal welfare and reduces the risk of disease. Manure management practices minimize environmental pollution.

By adopting GAP principles, farmers contribute to a safer, more responsible, and sustainable food system.

## 9.2 Pre-Harvest Handling and Storage Practices: Maintaining Freshness

Pre-harvest handling and storage practices play a critical role in preserving the quality, nutritional value, and freshness of agricultural produce from the field to the consumer's table. These practices directly impact the shelf life, nutritional value, and overall appearance of fruits, vegetables, and other agricultural products.

**Key Practices:**

**Field Sanitation:** Maintaining clean fields throughout the growing season is crucial to minimizing contamination by debris, weeds, or pathogens. This may involve practices like removing unwanted vegetation, managing irrigation water quality, and implementing proper sanitation protocols for farm equipment.

**Optimal Harvesting Time:** Harvesting crops at the peak of ripeness ensures optimal flavor, texture, and nutritional value. Indicators for optimal harvest timing may vary depending on the specific crop and may include factors like color, firmness, sugar content, or specific maturity stages.

**Immediate Cooling After Harvest:** Rapid cooling of harvested produce is essential to slow down the natural processes of respiration and deterioration. This can be achieved through methods like hydrocooling (chilling with water), forced-air cooling, or pre-cooling rooms. Prompt cooling helps maintain freshness, firmness, and shelf life.

**Appropriate Storage Conditions:** Providing proper storage facilities with controlled temperature, humidity, and ventilation is crucial for maintaining the quality, freshness, and shelf life of agricultural products. Optimal storage conditions vary depending on the specific crop, with some requiring cool and high-humidity environments, while others benefit from well-ventilated storage at room temperature.

**Challenges of Pre-Harvest Handling:**

**Small-Scale Farmers:** Limited access to cooling facilities or proper storage infrastructure can be a challenge for small-scale farmers, particularly in developing countries. Investing in basic cooling technologies or exploring community-based storage solutions can be crucial for these producers.

**Post-Harvest Losses:** Inadequate pre-harvest handling practices can lead to significant post-harvest losses, resulting in economic hardship for farmers and reduced availability of fresh produce for consumers. Investing in training for farmers on proper handling techniques and exploring cost-effective cooling solutions can help minimize these losses.

**Solutions for Pre-Harvest Handling Challenges:**

**Capacity Building:** Training programs for farmers on best practices for pre-harvest handling, including proper sanitation, harvesting techniques, and basic cooling methods, can significantly improve product quality and reduce losses.

**Technology Adoption:** Encouraging the adoption of appropriate technologies like portable cooling units or solar-powered drying systems can provide small-scale farmers with practical solutions for maintaining quality and extending shelf life.

**Collaboration and Infrastructure Development:** Facilitating collaboration among farmers and investing in shared storage facilities with proper cooling and ventilation can offer cost-effective solutions for small-scale producers.

## 9.3 Traceability in the Food Chain: Ensuring Transparency and Accountability

Food chain traceability involves monitoring and following the path of food products from production to distribution. This approach is crucial for guaranteeing food safety, expediting product recalls in instances of contamination, and fostering transparency within the food system.

**Key Elements of Traceability:**

**Identification and Labeling:** Each batch of agricultural products is assigned a unique identifier or label, such as a code or barcode. This label allows the product to be traced back to its origin, including the farm where it was produced.

**Record-Keeping:** Detailed records are maintained throughout the supply chain, documenting production practices, inputs used (seeds, fertilizers, pesticides), and the movement of products between different stages (farm, processing facility, distribution center, etc.).

**Technology-Enabled Traceability Systems:** Advanced technologies like barcodes, Radio Frequency Identification (RFID) tags, and blockchain offer efficient and reliable methods for tracking and tracing products throughout the supply chain. These technologies allow for real-time tracking and data collection, facilitating a faster response to food safety incidents.

**Regulatory Requirements:** Traceability regulations and standards are set by government agencies and international organizations to ensure food safety and quality control. Complying with these regulations is essential for all participants in the food chain.

**Benefits of Traceability Systems:**

**Enhanced Food Safety:** Traceability allows for quick and effective response to food safety incidents, enabling targeted product recalls and minimizing risks to consumers.

**Improved Consumer Confidence:** Consumers can gain greater confidence in the safety and origin of the food they purchase by knowing that products can be traced back to their source.

**Market Access:** Traceability systems can help farmers access premium markets that demand documented practices and responsible sourcing.

**Farmer Benefits:** Efficient traceability can help farmers identify areas for improvement in their practices, demonstrate responsible sourcing to buyers, and potentially command premium prices for their produce.

## *Case Study: Successful Traceability Implementation in Apple Production*

An association of apple farmers in a certain area established an extensive traceability system including barcodes and electronic data storage. This method enabled them to monitor each apple's journey from the orchard to the consumer, recording details such as the variety, harvest date, and precise handling procedures. The transparency boosted consumer confidence in the safety and origin of the apples and allowed the cooperative to quickly detect and resolve any potential quality issues. The established responsible practices enabled them to enter premium markets and sell their high-quality apples at a higher price.

Implementing efficient quality management procedures during the primary production phase helps farmers guarantee the safety, authenticity, and longevity of agricultural products. Implementing Good Agricultural Practices (GAP), effective pre-harvest handling and storage methods, and reliable traceability systems all enhance a responsible and sustainable food system that is advantageous for both producers and consumers.

## *Review Questions*

1. What are Good Agricultural Practices (GAP)?
2. Why are pre-harvest handling and storage practices important?
3. What is meant by traceability in the food chain?
4. How does GAP contribute to sustainable agriculture?
5. What factors should be considered in the pre-harvest handling of agricultural produce?
6. How does traceability contribute to food safety?
7. What are some examples of GAP in crop production?

8. How can proper storage practices affect the quality of agricultural produce?
9. What are the challenges in implementing traceability in the food chain?
10. How can technology aid in improving traceability in the food chain?

**Learning Activity:** Develop a GAP checklist for a specific crop production operation. Identify key GAP requirements related to soil management, water use, pesticide application, and harvest practices. Conduct an on-site assessment to evaluate compliance with GAP standards and recommend improvements to enhance product quality and safety.

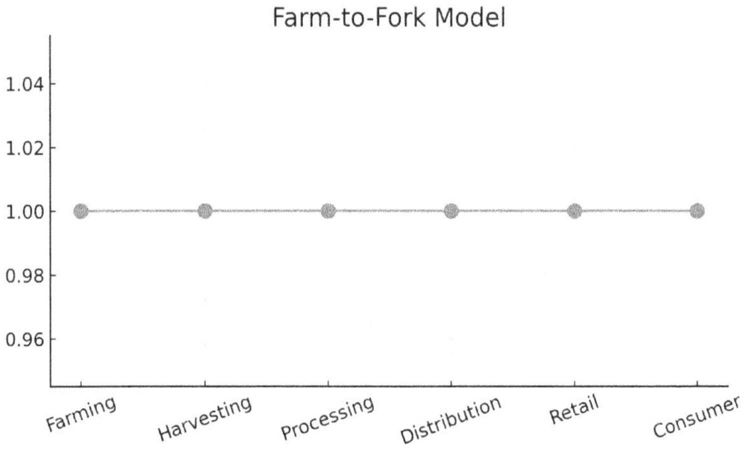


Farm to Fork

# CHAPTER X

# Quality Management in Food Processing

*""Precision and consistency are the silent architects of food excellence.""*

Ensuring the safety and quality of food throughout the processing chain is paramount. This chapter explores key quality management practices in food processing, including the application of Hazard Analysis and Critical Control Points (HACCP) principles, control of critical processing parameters, and the implementation of effective sanitation and hygiene practices within food processing plants.

## *10.1 Application of HACCP Principles*

The HACCP system is an internationally acknowledged method for reducing foodborne illness and assuring food safety during food processing.

**The following are the core principles of HACCP:**

HACCP is a proactive approach based on scientific principles that aims to pinpoint and manage potential risks that are likely to happen at certain stages in the food production process. It consists of seven fundamental principles:

**Conduct a Hazard Analysis:** Identify potential biological, chemical, and physical hazards associated with raw materials, ingredients, processing steps, and the finished product.

**Identify Critical Control Points (CCPs):** Identify critical control points in the processing chain to prevent, eliminate, or minimize hazards to acceptable levels.

**Establish Critical Limits for Each CCP:** Specify the exact conditions (such as temperature, time, pH) that need to be maintained at each Critical Control Point (CCP) to effectively manage identified dangers.

**Establish Monitoring Procedures:** Establish protocols for ongoing monitoring of Critical Control Points to confirm compliance with specified critical limits.

**Establish Corrective Actions:** Develop and document corrective actions to be taken if monitoring results indicate a deviation from critical limits.

**Verification Procedures:** Conduct periodic verification activities, such as internal audits, microbial testing, and equipment calibration, to confirm the effectiveness of the HACCP system.

**Record Keeping:** Maintain detailed records of all HACCP activities, including monitoring data, corrective actions taken, and verification results.

**Benefits of HACCP:**

**Proactive Approach:** HACCP focuses on preventing hazards rather than relying solely on end-product testing.

**Enhanced Food Safety:** By controlling hazards at critical points, HACCP minimizes the risk of foodborne illness associated with processed foods.

**International Recognition:** International food safety standards and regulations recognize HACCP, facilitating the trade of secure food products on a global scale.

**HACCP: Necessity and Advantages**

A comprehensive method of ensuring food safety is Hazard Analysis and Critical Control Point Production (HACCP), which identifies and manages physical, chemical, and biological hazards from the procurement of raw materials to the consumption of the final product. Managers must be totally dedicated to ensuring that a HACCP plan is successfully implemented and emphasize to workers the significance of maintaining food safety.

In the food business, HACCP is used in all areas, such as growing, harvesting, processing, manufacturing, marketing, selling, and making food for eating. Current Good Manufacturing Practices (cGMPs) and other prerequisite programs are necessary to build a strong foundation for making and implementing effective HACCP plans. Food preparation plants, stores that sell food, and places that serve food have all successfully put in place food safety systems that use HACCP ideas. These ideas are upheld by governments, trade groups, and the food industry around the world.

The food industry backs the idea of HACCP, which tells businesses they need to take an active part in making sure their food processing operations produce safe goods. The government uses its regulatory power to make sure that businesses have good HACCP plans and are following these plans correctly. This is different from regular government checks.

Instead of following a standard inspection process that wouldn't take into account how each business works and what makes each food product unique, HACCP lets companies focus on their own operations and unique qualities. Instead of focusing on a single production process, HACCP stresses the need for a tracking system to make sure that every business makes a safe product by lowering the risk of food safety problems.

**HACCP can generally be implemented with a 12-step process:**

1. Assemble a HACCP team.
2. Describe the food and its distribution.
3. Describe the intended use and consumers of the food.
4. Develop a flow diagram.
5. Conduct a hazard analysis.
6. Determine critical control points (CCPs).
7. Establish Critical Limits (CL)
8. Establish monitoring procedures.
9. Establish corrective actions.
10. Establish record-keeping procedures.
11. Establish verification procedures.
12. Establish procedures for evaluation and revision.

By reducing food safety risks effectively, this structured method makes sure that every business can make safe products. It gives businesses and food products the freedom to be flexible and change to their own specific needs. The goal is not on having a standard way to make things, but on having a way to keep an eye on things that is safe. This really shows how important HACCP is as a basic tool in the food business to keep food safe and of good quality.

## 10.2 Control of Critical Processing Parameters

Food processing involves various steps that can significantly impact the safety and quality of the final product. Controlling critical processing parameters at each stage is crucial for ensuring consistent quality and minimizing the risk of spoilage or contamination.

**Examples of Critical Processing Parameters:**

**Temperature Control:** Maintaining proper temperatures during processes like cooking, pasteurization, or freezing is essential for destroying pathogens and preserving product quality.

**Cooking Time:** Adequate cooking time at the appropriate temperature ensures the elimination of harmful bacteria and proper product texture.

**pH Levels:** Controlling the acidity or alkalinity (pH) of a product can inhibit the growth of certain microorganisms and influence product shelf-life.

**Water Activity (Aw):** Water activity (Aw) refers to the availability of free water in a product. Controlling AW can prevent microbial growth and extend its shelf life.

Effective monitoring and control of these critical processing parameters require the use of appropriate equipment, such as thermometers, timers, pH meters, and water activity meters. Regular calibration and maintenance of these instruments are essential for ensuring reliable data and consistent product quality.

## 10.3 Sanitation and Hygiene Practices in Food Processing Plants

Maintaining a clean and hygienic environment throughout the food processing facility is vital for preventing food contamination. This requires implementing and enforcing comprehensive sanitation and hygiene programs.

**Key Practices:**

**Plant Design and Layout:** Designing facilities with smooth, easily cleanable surfaces, proper ventilation, and adequate space for equipment and personnel movement promotes effective sanitation practices.

**Cleaning and Disinfection Procedures:** Establishing systematic cleaning and disinfection procedures for all equipment, surfaces, and utensils used in food processing helps prevent the spread of contamination.

**Pest Control Programs:** Having a full pest control program in place lowers the chance of rats, insects, and other pests spreading disease.

**Employee Hygiene Training:** Providing regular training for food handlers on proper hygiene practices, including handwashing, proper attire, and preventing contamination from personnel, is essential.

**Personal Protective Equipment (PPE):** Making workers wear the right PPE, like hairnets, gloves, and aprons, lowers the chance that food will get contaminated.

**Maintaining a Culture of Food Safety:**

Effective sanitation and hygiene programs are most successful when supported by a strong culture of food safety within the food processing plant. Management commitment to food safety principles, along with ongoing employee training and communication, are essential for ensuring consistent adherence to sanitation protocols. By implementing a comprehensive quality management system that incorporates HACCP principles, control of critical processing parameters, and effective sanitation,

HACCP, or Hazard Analysis and Critical Control Points, is a proactive approach to food safety in the food processing industry. It involves conducting a hazard analysis, identifying critical control points, establishing limits, monitoring procedures, corrective actions, and maintaining records. This approach minimizes foodborne illness and ensures consistent quality throughout the food production chain. Implementing a comprehensive quality management system is crucial

## *Review Questions*

1. What are the seven principles of HACCP?
2. How does controlling critical processing parameters contribute to food safety and quality?
3. What are some examples of critical processing parameters in food processing?
4. Why are sanitation and hygiene important in food processing plants?
5. What are some key practices for maintaining sanitation and hygiene in food processing plants?
6. How does a strong culture of food safety support effective sanitation and hygiene programs?
7. How does the HACCP system enhance food safety?
8. What are the benefits of implementing a comprehensive quality management system in food processing?
9. How can equipment like thermometers, timers, pH meters, and water activity meters aid in controlling critical processing parameters?
10. What role does record keeping play in the HACCP system?

**Learning Activity:** Develop a HACCP plan for a specific food processing operation. Identify potential hazards associated with the processing steps, establish critical control points, determine monitoring procedures, and develop corrective actions to address deviations from critical limits. Conduct a risk assessment to evaluate the effectiveness of the HACCP plan in controlling food safety hazards.

# CHAPTER XI

# Quality Management Tools and Techniques

*"Data-driven decisions transform assumptions into assurance."*

Making sure that the quality of food output stays high is essential for success. This chapter talks about different quality management tools and methods that can help food companies be more productive, make customers happier, stay ahead of the competition, and build a loyal customer base. By learning how to use these tools correctly, food businesses can find and fix quality problems, make processes run more smoothly, and finally give customers safe, high-quality goods.

## 11.1 Importance of Quality Management Tools

Quality management tools are not mere fads; they are powerful instruments that provide valuable insights and facilitate continuous improvement in food production. Here's how these tools contribute to success:

**Higher Productivity Levels:** By identifying bottlenecks and inefficiencies in processes through tools like flowcharts, manufacturers can optimize production flow, leading to increased output and reduced waste.

**Improved Customer Satisfaction:** Tools like Pareto charts help prioritize quality improvement efforts based on customer concerns, leading to products that better meet consumer expectations and enhance satisfaction.

**A Competitive Edge in the Market:** Consistent product quality, which can be achieved with tools like control charts and good quality control, gives manufacturers an edge over their rivals and a place in the market.

**A Loyal Customer Base:** Delivering safe and reliable products fosters trust and loyalty among consumers, leading to a strong and dependable customer base.

**Identifying Cause-and-Effect Relationships:** Tools like cause-and-effect diagrams (Ishikawa diagrams) help pinpoint the root causes of quality issues, allowing for targeted corrective actions and preventing future occurrences.

## *11.2 Quality Management Tools*

**Flowchart:** A flowchart illustrates the necessary actions, decision points, and potential outcomes. Flowcharts aid in visualizing the process, identifying potential issues or areas for improvement, and enhancing communication and comprehension within a team. A flowchart can illustrate the complete food production process, starting from obtaining the raw materials to packing the final product. This image can assist in identifying locations susceptible to contamination, inefficient handling, or sluggish processing.

We are all familiar with the term "flowchart" from our educational experiences. Flowcharts are visual representations that illustrate a sequence of steps, a formula, or a procedure. The diagrams consist of lines with arrows pointing in various ways to link the distinct stages.

Flowcharts illustrate the organizational structure, login processes, document workflows, billing transactions, and other procedures inside an organization.

A flowchart provides a visual representation of the sequence of events in a system.

This step of the process involves providing information or a visual representation of how the process functions. This will also aid in resolving any quality issues. A flowchart can assist in identifying the specific stage within the process where the quality issue is occurring.

Each step in this process is an activity that produces a result, which is then inputted into the following phase.

Below is a flowchart depicting the layout of the kitchen in a five-star hotel.

The flowchart illustrates the operational framework of the kitchen department in a five-star hotel.

**Histogram:** A histogram is a visual representation of data distribution that shows how often distinct values occur in a collection. Histograms help identify trends in data, such as fluctuations in product weight, variations in temperature, or discrepancies in shelf life. This enables the timely identification of possible quality concerns. A histogram might be utilized in food manufacturing to examine the weight distribution of packaged cookies, guaranteeing uniform product fill and avoiding underfilling or overfilling.

- One common way to show and study the spread of a dataset visually is with a histogram. By finding the frequency of data within a certain area, it shows the shape of the distribution.
- The spread between the lowest and highest observations is split into equal parts to make a histogram.
- Counting the number of readings in each interval gives the frequency, which is then shown on the graph as the height of a bar.
- The basic data distribution can be shown more simply with the help of the histogram.

**Instructions:** Step 1: Collect miscellaneous data, such length, distance, weight, and time.

Step 2: Convert the graph into a histogram. You can accomplish this manually or by using an application.

Step 3: Formulate your opinion.

**Components of a histogram:**

Name: The graph's information is elucidated in the title.

Axis X: The X-axis displays the range of numbers within which the measurements are categorized.

The vertical axis: The Y-axis displays the frequency of values falling inside the specified ranges on the X-axis.

These bars: The width of the bar represents the range of values displayed, and the height of the bar indicates the frequency of each value occurring within the range. Each bar in a histogram with equally sized bins should have uniform thickness.

Jeff manages a local bank branch. Customers have been complaining to Jeff about extended waiting times to receive assistance from customer service representatives. Jeff opts to observe each customer's waiting time and record it. These are the lessons he acquired by observing and recording the duration of waiting times for 20 individuals:

**Cause-and-Effect Chart (Ishikawa Diagram):** The fishbone diagram, sometimes called Ishikawa diagram, is a tool used to discover the root causes of a quality problem by categorizing contributing elements into major areas such as methods, materials, machines, people, measurement, and environment (MMMEDM). The Ishikawa diagram encourages a methodical problem-solving approach by enabling a thorough investigation of the possible reasons of a quality issue. This enables specific corrective measures instead of relying on speculation. This method can be utilized in food manufacturing to pinpoint the underlying reason for a sudden surge in consumer complaints regarding the burnt taste of crackers. By analyzing parameters associated with MMMEDM, it was determined that a defective oven heating element in the machines category was causing irregular baking temperatures.

- The Cause-Effect diagram is occasionally called a "fish bone diagram" because of its visual similarity to the lateral perspective of a fish skeleton. Each member of the problem-solving team possesses a unique viewpoint regarding the fundamental origin of the problem.

- Using the brainstorming technique, the fishbone diagram exhaustively identifies all causes and concepts, focusing on the most critical fundamental cause.
- Causes and effects diagrams are graphical representations that detail the origins of specific challenges or problems that arise in relation to the processing system. There are numerous contributors to a particular issue.
- Commence the fishbone analysis by articulating the problem at hand as a query, employing the "why" format in particular. Having answers prepared for each query will facilitate the process of generating ideas. In the end, a consensus should be achieved by the entire team regarding the problem statement, after which this inquiry should be prioritized in the fishbone diagram.
- A horizontal line connects the problem statement at the top of the fishbone diagram to the branching vertical lines that resemble bones.

For instance, at 4:00 PM, a hotel manager may wish to determine why guest rooms are not prepared for check-in. The manager collaborates with the enhancement team to generate reasons and classifies them using a cause-and-effect diagram. The group can subsequently establish enhancement suggestions and prioritize problem areas.

**Scatter Diagram:** A scatter diagram is a visual depiction that illustrates the correlation between two variables through the arrangement of data points in the form of plotted coordinates. Scatter diagrams are helpful for identifying trends or correlations between variables. As an illustration, a correlation between the shelf life of yogurt and storage temperature could be unveiled using a scatter diagram. A scatter diagram may be utilized in food production to examine the correlation between the quantity of salt incorporated during the baking process of bread and the ultimate firmness of the product. This can assist producers in achieving a uniform texture by optimizing salt levels.

- Scatter diagrams visually depict the correlation between variables. Variables often represent possible causes and outcomes.
- A scatter diagram could show the association between volunteers' satisfaction levels during orientation training.
- The graphic illustrates the correlation between volunteer satisfaction ratings and volunteer orientation training.

## *11.3 Additional Tools*

**Checklist:** A checklist is a standardized list of steps or procedures that need to be followed to ensure a task is completed correctly and consistently. Checklists reduce errors by ensuring essential steps are completed, especially in tasks related to sanitation, equipment maintenance, and quality control inspections.

- A check sheet is a fundamental quality tool utilized for data collection. Check sheets can monitor the occurrence rate of particular events.
- Check sheets gather data in a format that is easy for users to understand.
- It enhances precision in the data collection process through simple procedures and formats. It greatly minimizes the amount of work needed for data collection. Check sheet data collecting is based on actual data rather than theoretical figures.
- Marks or checks are recorded on the check sheet to update it. The Human Resource Department monitors the daily amount of inquiries raised in various categories in the following example.

The table below displays the total number of inquiries raised in the Human Department categorized by health insurance, sick leave, paid time off, etc. The tool also offers data on the overall number of inquiries made each day of the week.

**Pareto Chart:** A Pareto chart, also referred to as the 80/20 rule, is a bar graph that illustrates the most common reasons (usually responsible for 80% of the issue) and the least common causes (responsible for the remaining 20%). Pareto charts assist in prioritizing quality improvement endeavors by emphasizing the areas with the most substantial influence on addressing a quality problem. This enables the allocation of resources to the most crucial factors.

- A Pareto chart is a bar graph that displays data from the highest to the lowest frequencies.
- Pareto analysis follows the 80/20 rule, where a small number of factors typically have the most significant impact.
- 80% of sales are generated by 20% of customers.
- 80% of faults stem from 20% of underlying causes.
- The distribution may not be precisely 80/20, but you will notice that a small number of crucial factors have a significant impact.
- It is straightforward in its approach.
- The data is shown in a bar chart where the frequency or impact is displayed in descending order alongside specific cause codes or causes for failure or issues.
- This strategy allows you to promptly identify the most significant effects of a select few crucial factors.
- Once you have this information, you can start enhancing the crucial fundamental reasons.

We are analyzing the number of product defects in each category in this particular sample. By examining the faults in descending order of frequency, it becomes clear how to prioritize improvement initiatives. Prioritize addressing the most prominent issues first.

**Control Chart:** A control chart is a statistical instrument utilized for monitoring process stability and identifying deviations from predetermined quality benchmarks. The display usually shows the mean value of a quality measure over time, as well as statistically computed upper and lower control limits (UCL and LCL) based on previous data. Control charts enable the continuous monitoring of essential process variables, like temperature in pasteurization or pH levels in yogurt manufacturing. Deviation beyond control limits signals possible quality issues necessitating prompt examination and corrective measures.

Control charts, which are alternatively referred to as run charts, visually represent the progression of data points in chronological order to depict its trend.

The data are depicted in the charts in a consistent manner, with the frequency of high or low outliers indicated.

The focus is on the surveillance of performance trends through the examination of data point fluctuations. It discerns variations resulting from special causes as opposed to common causes. The Dow Jones Industrial Average functions as a model control chart in and of itself.

## 11.4 Case Study: Effective Use of a Quality Management Tool

A bakery was experiencing customer complaints about inconsistent cake sizes and uneven baking. To identify the root cause, they employed a cause-and-effect chart (Ishikawa diagram). By brainstorming factors related to MMMEDM categories, they identified a potential culprit in the "machines" category. Further investigation revealed a malfunctioning batter dispenser that was depositing uneven amounts of batter into cake pans. By repairing the dispenser and implementing a control chart to monitor batter weight, the bakery resolved the size inconsistency issue. Additionally, a review of oven temperatures (machines category) and baking times (methods category) led to adjustments that ensured even baking and eliminated customer complaints.

This case study demonstrates how effectively using a quality management tool, like the Ishikawa diagram, can pinpoint the root cause of a quality issue, leading to corrective actions and improved product consistency.

## *Review Questions*

1. What are the benefits of using quality management tools in food production?
2. How can a flowchart be used in a food production process?
3. What insights can a histogram provide in the context of food quality?
4. How can an Ishikawa diagram help in identifying the root cause of a quality issue?
5. What is the purpose of a scatter diagram in analyzing food quality data?
6. How can a checklist contribute to quality assurance in food production?
7. What is the 80/20 rule in a Pareto chart, and how can it be applied to prioritizing quality improvement efforts?
8. How does a control chart aid in monitoring process stability in food production?
9. In the given case study, how did the bakery use the Ishikawa diagram and control chart to resolve their quality issue?
10. Can you think of a situation in food production where a quality management tool can be effectively applied? Describe the situation and the chosen tool.

**Learning Activity:** Conduct a group exercise where students analyze a simulated quality issue using various quality management tools. Each group can select a different tool and present their findings, highlighting the tool's effectiveness in problem-solving and decision-making.

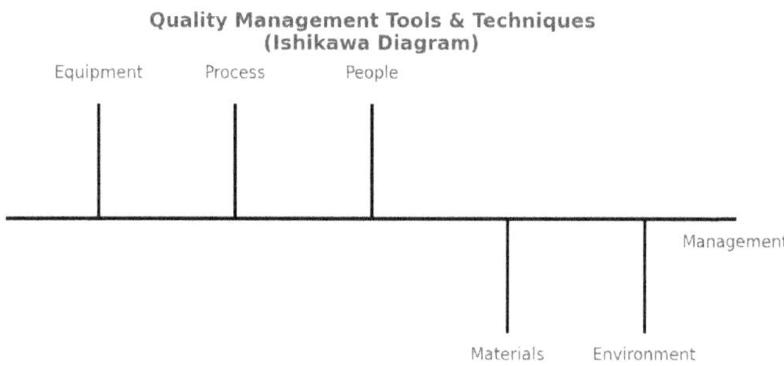


Ishikawa Diagram

# CHAPTER XII

# Food Safety and Quality in the Global Market

*"*"In a connected world, food safety is not just local responsibility—it's a global commitment."*"*

A wide variety of options are available on the global food market, as products must cross continents in order to reach consumers. The state of interconnectivity, although bestowing advantages, also presents distinctive obstacles in the realm of food safety and quality.

## 12.1 Impact of Globalization on Food Safety Concerns

Globalization has significantly transformed the food supply chain, bringing both advantages and challenges.

**Increased Trade and Diverse Choices:** Globalization has facilitated a significant increase in international food trade, offering consumers a wider variety of food products from around the world. This diversity enriches culinary experiences and provides access to exotic ingredients.

**Lengthening Supply Chains:** The sourcing of ingredients and finished products from across the globe has resulted in longer and more intricate supply chains. This complexity makes it more challenging to trace the origin of food products and ensure consistent adherence to safety standards throughout the chain.

**Regulatory Disparities:** Food safety regulations and enforcement practices vary considerably between countries. This inconsistency can create confusion for businesses operating internationally and make it difficult to guarantee uniform safety standards for products entering the global market.

**Emerging Food Safety Risks:** Globalization has inadvertently facilitated the spread of foodborne pathogens, contaminants, and diseases. Products carrying these risks can travel long distances, potentially leading to widespread outbreaks if left undetected.

**Heightened Consumer Awareness:** Increased access to information and heightened consumer awareness have raised expectations for transparency and accountability in the global food market. Consumers demand to know the origin, safety standards, and potential risks associated with the food they purchase.

International collaboration is essential to addressing these challenges. Harmonization of food safety regulations across countries, along with robust risk assessment and management strategies, is crucial for safeguarding the integrity of the global food supply.

## 12.2 *Food Import/Export Regulations and Standards: Safeguarding the Global Food Chain*

Food import and export regulations and standards are critical instruments in ensuring the safety and quality of food products that traverse international borders, promoting fair trade, and safeguarding public health. It is crucial to take into account the following:

**Compliance with International Standards:** Countries engaged in import and export activities are obligated to comply with regulations and standards that have been established by international organizations such as the Codex Alimentarius Commission, the World Health Organization (WHO), and the Food and Agriculture Organization (FAO). These organizations advocate for consumer protection, international food safety standard harmonization, and consistency.

**Inspection and Certification Processes:** Competent authorities in importing countries may subject food products to inspections, testing, and certification procedures. These procedures verify compliance with regulatory requirements, including sanitary and phytosanitary measures (addressing plant and animal health risks), labeling accuracy, and packaging standards.

**Risk-Based Approach:** Regulatory frameworks often employ risk-based approaches to assess and manage the safety risks associated with imported and exported food products. When determining the level of scrutiny, factors such as the nature of the product, its country of origin, the production practices employed, and the nation's previous compliance history are all taken into account.

**Traceability and Transparency:** Establishing and implementing robust traceability systems throughout the supply chain is paramount. Traceability allows for tracking and tracing food products at every stage, from farm to fork. This transparency facilitates targeted recalls in cases of food safety incidents and enhances consumer confidence in the global food system.

International cooperation, through mechanisms like mutual recognition agreements (where countries recognize each other's inspection and certification systems) and capacity building initiatives (supporting developing countries in implementing robust food safety protocols), can significantly contribute to smoother trade and ensure the safety and quality of food products in the global market.

## 12.3 Food Fraud and Adulteration: Threats to Food Integrity

Food fraud and adulteration have severe consequences, undermining consumer trust, jeopardizing public health, and distorting fair market competition. These illegal practices encompass a range of activities aimed at deceiving consumers about the authenticity, origin, quality, or safety of food products:

**Economic Motivation:** The primary driver of food fraud is often economic gain. Unethical actors may resort to practices like diluting products with cheaper ingredients, substituting higher-quality components with lower-cost alternatives, or mislabeling products to increase profits or reduce production costs.

**Detecting food fraud schemes can be intricate and challenging due to their complexity.** Sophisticated analytical techniques, robust surveillance systems, and close collaboration between industry, government agencies, and academic institutions are required to identify and mitigate these risks.

**Consumer Deception:** Food fraud undermines consumer trust in the food supply chain. Consumers are misled into purchasing products that may not be what they appear to be, potentially posing health risks or failing to meet their expectations regarding quality and origin.

**Regulatory Response:** Governments and regulatory bodies are

## *Review Questions*

1. How has globalization impacted food safety concerns?
2. What are the key considerations in food import/export regulations and standards?
3. How do food fraud and adulteration threaten food integrity?
4. What role do international organizations play in harmonizing food safety standards?
5. How does a risk-based approach aid in managing safety risks associated with imported and exported food products?
6. Why is traceability important in the global food supply chain?
7. What motivates actors to engage in food fraud?
8. What challenges are faced in detecting food fraud?
9. How does food fraud impact consumer trust in the food supply chain?
10. How can regulatory bodies effectively combat food fraud and adulteration?

**Learning Activity:** Organize a debate on the topic of food globalization and its impact on food safety. Assign students to argue for or against the motion, considering factors such as regulatory challenges, cultural differences, and technological advancements.

Divide students into groups and assign each group a specific aspect of global food safety (e.g., import/export regulations, food fraud prevention). Ask them to conduct research and create presentations summarizing their findings, including challenges, best practices, and recommendations for improvement.

## BASIC TASTES:
## SWEET, SALTY, SOUR, BITTER & UMAMI

Western contemporary science recognizes only these as five basic tastes as these are captured on our tongue.

Can these describe the taste of all the elements of a portion of *Aloo-gobhi*?

Can these describe taste of turmeric, garlic, ginger, spices, chillies, *jamuns*, *amlas*, or roasted chana?

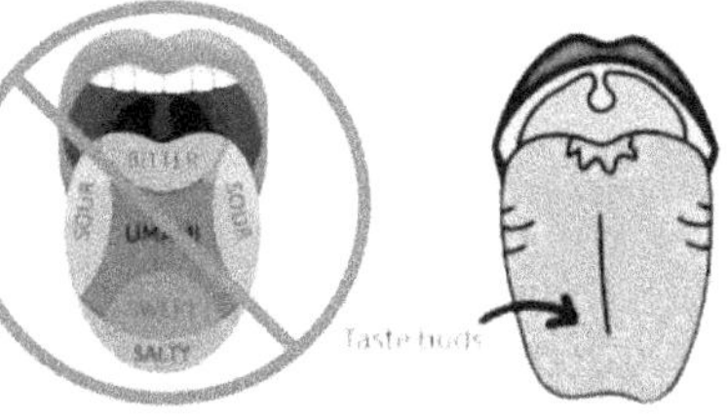


Basic Taste

# CHAPTER XIII

# New Technologies for Food Quality Assurance

*""The future depends on what we do in the present." — Mahatma Gandhi"*

Technological progress is currently transforming the food industry, significantly impacting the domain of food quality management. This chapter explores three innovative technologies that are significantly transforming food quality assurance: biosensors, which enable rapid detection of pathogens; non-destructive methods for assessing food quality; and the promising uses of artificial intelligence (AI) within the food sector.

## *13.1 Biosensors for Foodborne Pathogen Detection: Enhancing Safety Checks*

Biosensors are analytical devices that integrate biological components with transducers to detect target analytes rapidly and accurately. Here's a closer look at the key advantages of biosensors:

**Rapid Detection:** Biosensors offer swift detection of foodborne pathogens, ensuring timely intervention to prevent foodborne illness outbreaks.

**Enhanced Sensitivity and Specificity:** They can accurately detect pathogens even at low concentrations, reducing the risk of false results.

**On-Site Testing Capabilities:** Portable biosensors enable on-site testing, empowering stakeholders to make informed decisions about food safety.

**Multiplexing Potential:** Advanced biosensors can detect multiple pathogens simultaneously, improving efficiency in food safety testing.

For instance, a biosensor utilizing DNA aptamers swiftly identifies Salmonella in poultry, enabling timely interventions to prevent contamination outbreaks and ensuring the safety of consumers.

## 13.2 Non-Destructive Techniques for Food Quality Evaluation

Non-destructive techniques enable the evaluation of food quality without altering the product itself, ensuring its integrity is maintained. Key advantages include:

Preservation of Product Integrity: Non-destructive techniques allow for quality evaluation without compromising the product's physical, chemical, or sensory properties.

Real-Time Monitoring: These techniques enable continuous monitoring of quality parameters, facilitating proactive adjustments during processing and storage.

Cost-Effectiveness: Reduced sample preparation and waste generation translate to cost savings for producers.

Automation and Integration: Integration into automated inspection systems enhances efficiency and consistency in quality control.

For instance, near-infrared spectroscopy (NIRS) offers rapid and precise assessments of critical quality metrics such as moisture, fat, and protein content in food products, enabling producers to maintain quality standards without affecting the integrity of the items.

## 13.3 Applications of Artificial Intelligence in Food Quality Management

Artificial intelligence (AI) technologies leverage data to optimize various aspects of food quality management. Key applications include:

- Predictive Modeling: AI predicts food quality parameters, facilitating proactive quality control measures.
- Quality Control Optimization: Real-time monitoring and adjustment of production processes maintain consistent quality.
- Fraud Detection: AI analyzes data to detect instances of food fraud, enhancing transparency and trust.
- Personalized Nutrition: AI recommends personalized food products and dietary plans based on individual preferences and health data.
- Real-World Example: AI-based image recognition systems identify defects and deviations from quality parameters on food processing lines, ensuring consistent product quality.

In summary, the integration of biosensors, non-destructive techniques, and AI is transforming food quality assurance, playing a pivotal role in bolstering safety, efficiency, and consumer confidence across the global food supply chain.

## *Review Questions:*

1. What are biosensors, and how do they contribute to food safety?

2. Explain the advantages of non-destructive techniques in food quality evaluation.

3. How does artificial intelligence optimize food quality management?

4. Provide an example of a biosensor application in the food industry.

5. Describe the real-world application of near-infrared spectroscopy (NIRS) in food quality evaluation.

6. Discuss the importance of real-time monitoring in food quality control.

7. How does AI contribute to fraud detection in the food supply chain?

8. Explain the concept of personalized nutrition and its relevance to AI in the food industry.

9. What are the key benefits of using AI-based image recognition systems in food processing?

10. How do these new technologies collectively contribute to enhancing food safety and quality in the global market?

**Learning Activity:** Divide students into small groups and assign each group a specific technology discussed in the chapter (e.g., biosensors, AI). Ask them to prepare a short presentation highlighting the technology's principles, applications, and potential impact on food quality assurance.

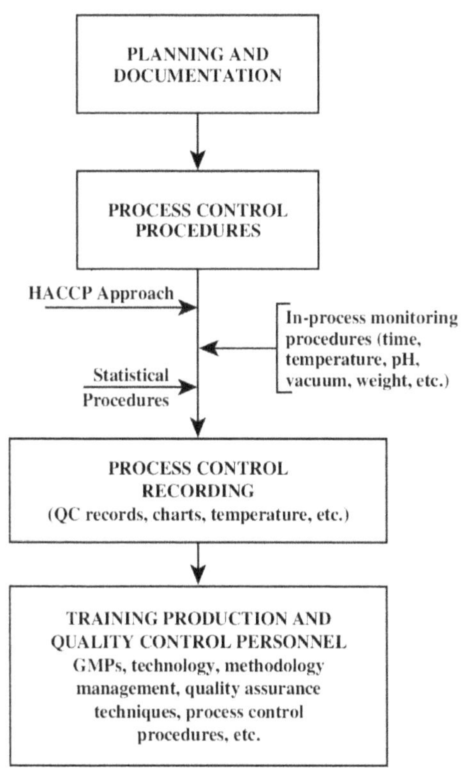

# Quality Assurance for the Food Industry

84

# CHAPTER XIV

# The Future of Food Quality Management

*"*"The future of food is built on today's commitment to quality and sustainability."*"*

The landscape of food quality management is undergoing a dynamic transformation, driven by a confluence of emerging trends and innovative technologies.

## 14.1 Sustainable Food Production and Quality: A Holistic Approach

Sustainable food production practices prioritize environmental responsibility, social equity, and economic viability throughout the food supply chain. Consumers' deeper understanding of the connections between sustainable production methods, food quality, and overall well-being highlights the increasing integration of this holistic approach with food quality.

**Environmental Impact:** Sustainable practices minimize the environmental footprint of food production. For instance, sustainable practices may include reducing reliance on synthetic chemicals, conserving water resources, and promoting biodiversity. By minimizing environmental impact, sustainable practices can contribute to healthier soil, cleaner water, and a more balanced ecosystem, which can positively influence the quality and nutritional content of food products.

**Supporting Local Economies:** Sustainable food production often emphasizes local sourcing and supporting local farmers and producers. This fosters stronger community connections, ensures the availability of fresher ingredients, and can result in higher quality and better-tasting food products.

**Animal Welfare:** Sustainable practices promote the ethical treatment of animals raised for food. This includes providing animals with humane living conditions and access to natural behaviors, which can enhance meat quality and contribute to the overall well-being of the animals.

**Real-World Example:** Research has indicated that fruits and vegetables produced through organic farming methods, which abstain from the use of synthetic fertilizers and pesticides, may contain greater concentrations of specific phytonutrients and antioxidants in comparison to produce cultivated using conventional methods. This serves as an illustration of the possible correlation between sustainable agricultural practices and better nutritional content in food.

## 14.2 Consumer Demands and Trends in Food Quality: A More Discerning Marketplace

Consumer preferences and expectations are a powerful driving force in shaping the future of food quality management.

**Focus on Health and Nutrition:** Consumers are increasingly seeking out food products that are not only delicious but also promote good health and well-being. This encompasses an increasing preference for products that are minimally processed, nutrient-rich, and devoid of artificial additives or preservatives.

**Ethical Concerns:** Consumers are becoming more mindful of the ethical implications of their food choices. This includes interest in animal welfare, fair labor practices throughout the supply chain, and environmental sustainability considerations during production.

**Transparency and Traceability:** Consumers desire to know the origin, production method, and route of their food before it reaches their tables. The establishment of consumer confidence and the promotion of trust in the food supply chain are contingent upon the implementation of traceability and increased transparency.

**Real-World Example:** The rise in popularity of plant-based and cruelty-free food options reflects a growing consumer interest in ethical sourcing and production practices. This trend indicates a transformation in consumer values, leading to a demand for food products that resonate with their ethical beliefs.

## 14.3 *The Role of Blockchain Technology in Food Traceability: A Secure and Transparent Journey*

Initially designed for cryptocurrencies, blockchain technology is now transforming the food traceability industry. A digital ledger system, blockchain enables the recording of transactions in a secure, transparent, and tamper-proof manner. It holds promise for the future of food quality management in the following ways:

**Enhanced Traceability:** Blockchain can track the movement of food products from farm to fork, recording every step of the journey. This detailed record-keeping allows for pinpointing the origin, processing history, and current location of any food item, enhancing transparency and accountability within the supply chain.

**Improved Food Safety:** By providing a secure and immutable record of food handling practices, blockchain can help identify potential contamination points and facilitate swift recalls in case of food safety incidents. This rapid response capability can minimize the risks associated with contaminated food products.

**Reduced Food Fraud:** Blockchain's tamper-proof nature makes it difficult to alter or falsify data within the system. This can help reduce instances of food fraud, such as mislabeling or substituting ingredients, bolstering consumer trust in the authenticity and quality of food products.

**Real-World Example:** Several companies are already implementing blockchain technology to track the journey of seafood from the time it's caught in the ocean to when it arrives at restaurants. This ensures that the seafood is sustainably sourced, properly handled during transportation and storage, and ultimately delivered to consumers with a verifiable record of its origin and quality.

In conclusion, the future of food quality management is characterized by a holistic approach that considers environmental and social responsibility alongside traditional quality metrics. By embracing sustainable practices, responding to evolving consumer demands, and leveraging innovative technologies like blockchain, the food industry can ensure a future with safe, high-quality, and ethically produced food for all.

## *Review Questions*

1. What is sustainable food production, and how does it relate to food quality?
2. How are consumer demands influencing trends in food quality management?
3. What is blockchain technology, and how can it be used to improve food traceability?
4. Give a real-world example of how sustainable food production practices can enhance food quality.
5. Discuss a trend in consumer demand that is currently shaping food quality management practices.
6. How can blockchain technology enhance food safety and reduce fraud?
7. What are some potential benefits of using blockchain technology in food quality management?
8. How might consumer demands for food quality evolve in the future?
9. What are some challenges and opportunities for food quality management in the context of sustainable food production?
10. How might new technologies like blockchain transform the future of food quality management?

**Learning Activity:** Organize a debate or panel discussion on the future of food quality management, inviting industry experts, policymakers, and academics to share their insights on emerging trends, challenges, and strategies for sustainable food production and quality assurance.

Our Food System

# CHAPTER XV

# Quality Leadership in Food Management

*"*"A leader in food quality doesn't demand excellence but demonstrates it.""*

Within the realm of food management, achieving and maintaining a consistent focus on quality hinges on effective leadership. This chapter delves into the critical role of quality leadership, exploring strategies for motivating employees, building strong teams, recognizing valuable contributions, and fostering employee involvement in quality initiatives.

## 15.1 The Cornerstone of Quality: Effective Leadership

Quality leadership serves as the cornerstone for establishing and upholding a culture of quality within food management systems. Leaders play a pivotal role in shaping the organizational culture, setting clear quality objectives, and providing guidance and support to ensure adherence to established quality standards. Here's a breakdown of their key responsibilities:

**Setting the Tone:** Leaders have a significant impact on the organizational culture as a whole through their dedication to quality and ongoing progress, which serves as a model for the entire team.

**Defining Quality Objectives:** Leaders convert the overarching vision of the organization into quantifiable, transparent quality goals. By adhering to the SMART criteria—specific, attainable, relevant, and time-bound—these objectives will serve as a guide for efficiently attaining quality-related goals.

**Providing Direction and Support:** Leaders provide clear direction and ongoing support to employees at all levels. This includes ensuring employees have the necessary resources, training, and guidance to effectively implement quality initiatives.

**Leading by Example:** Leaders demonstrate their commitment to quality through their actions and behaviors. This can involve actively participating in quality improvement initiatives, role-modeling desired behaviors, and holding themselves accountable for upholding quality standards.

## 15.2 Building a Quality-Driven Workforce: Strategies for Motivation

A motivated workforce is essential for achieving quality objectives in food management. Here are key strategies for fostering motivation among employees:

Setting clear and achievable goals for individuals and teams gives them a clear feeling of purpose and direction. Recognizing and rewarding employees who surpass these goals or show exceptional commitment to quality helps reinforce positive behavior and encourages ongoing excellence.

Encouraging initiative and granting employees liberty and responsibility to make decisions and take ownership for excellent outcomes promotes accountability.

Efficient Communication and Feedback: It is crucial to sustain transparent communication channels to cultivate a culture of excellence in an organization. To foster staff growth, leaders should practice active listening, provide constructive feedback, and ensure clear communication of high-quality goals and expectations.

Offering professional development opportunities, such training programs, that enhance the skills and knowledge of employees in quality management methods helps them make more effective contributions to quality-related projects.

## 15.3 Building Effective Teams for Quality Success

High-performing teams are the backbone of achieving quality objectives in food management systems. Here's how to build effective teams:

**Fostering Collaboration:** Creating a collaborative environment where team members share ideas, work together to solve problems, and support each other is essential for achieving quality goals.

**Promoting Diversity:** Having diversity in skills, backgrounds, and perspectives within teams not only fosters creativity but also leads to more comprehensive solutions for addressing quality improvement challenges.

**Clear Roles and Responsibilities:** Clearly defined roles and responsibilities for each team member ensure everyone understands their specific contributions to achieving quality objectives. This minimizes confusion and fosters accountability.

**Culture of Trust and Accountability:** Establishing a culture of trust and accountability within teams empowers members to mutually hold each other responsible for maintaining quality standards and reaching shared objectives.

## 15.4 Recognizing and Rewarding Contributions

Recognizing and rewarding employee contributions to quality improvement efforts reinforces a culture of quality and motivates continued engagement.

**Verbal Praise:** Public recognition in team meetings or personal notes from supervisors expressing appreciation for a job well done can be highly motivating and demonstrate that employee contributions are valued.

**Awards and Incentives:** Employee of the Month recognition or performance bonuses tied to quality metrics can provide tangible recognition and encourage continued commitment to quality.

**Career Advancement Opportunities:** Providing opportunities for professional growth and advancement for employees who consistently demonstrate a commitment to quality can be a powerful motivator.

## *15.5 Employee Involvement*

Employee involvement in quality initiatives is a key ingredient for success in food management systems. Here are the benefits of fostering employee involvement:

**Improved Morale and Job Satisfaction:** Employees who feel valued and have the opportunity to contribute to meaningful initiatives, such as implementing a new customer feedback system that improves satisfaction rates, experience a greater sense of ownership and satisfaction in their work.

**Enhanced Problem-Solving and Innovation:** A diverse range of perspectives and ideas from employees across various levels of the organization can lead to more creative solutions for quality challenges and foster continuous improvement.

**Increased Productivity and Efficiency:** Engaged employees, such as those who suggested a new inventory management system that reduced waste by 20%, are more invested in achieving quality objectives and are more likely to identify and implement efficiencies within processes.

**Stronger Customer Focus:** When employees are involved in quality initiatives, they gain a deeper understanding of the importance of meeting customer needs and expectations, leading to a more customer-centric approach within the organization.

## *Review Questions*

1. What is the role of effective leadership in establishing and upholding a culture of quality within food management systems?
2. How do leaders convert the overarching vision of the organization into quantifiable, transparent quality goals?
3. Discuss the key strategies for fostering motivation among employees in the food management sector.

4. How does setting clear and achievable goals for individuals and teams contribute to a quality-driven workforce?
5. What are the benefits of fostering a collaborative environment and promoting diversity within teams in achieving quality objectives?
6. How does recognizing and rewarding employee contributions reinforce a culture of quality and motivate continued engagement?
7. Discuss the benefits of fostering employee involvement in quality initiatives.
8. How does employee involvement lead to enhanced problem-solving and innovation in food management systems?
9. How can engaged employees contribute to increased productivity and efficiency in food management systems?
10. How does employee involvement in quality initiatives lead to a stronger customer focus within the organization?

**Learning Activity:** Conduct a leadership development workshop where students role-play different leadership scenarios related to food quality management. Encourage them to apply leadership theories and techniques to address common challenges and opportunities faced by quality leaders in the food industry.

Common Leadership Styles

# CHAPTER XVI

# Food Laws and Regulations

*"Regulations set the standard, but ethical responsibility defines the legacy."""*

In the food industry, following legal criteria is crucial to upholding customer safety and quality standards. This chapter examines the legal and regulatory frameworks that control food quality and safety, including the internationally known Codex Alimentarius, the Essential Commodities Act, the Agricultural Produce (Grading and Marketing) Act, and the Prevention of Food Adulteration Act.

## 16.1 Prevention of Food Adulteration Act, 1954 (PFA)

Enacted in 1954, the Prevention of Food Adulteration Act aims to outlaw the adulteration of food and establish guidelines for food safety. To guarantee careful supervision of food safety, the regulations cover a number of topics, including food additives, preservatives, coloring agents, packaging, and labeling. The act lays out guidelines for analysis, sampling, and the penalties for violations.

## 16.2 Essential Commodities Act, 1955

Food and other essential commodities are produced, traded, and distributed under the authority of the important Commodities Act of 1955. Under this law, control orders, such as the Fruit Product Order and Meat Products Control Orders, ensure hygienic requirements and standards of quality in the production and distribution of food.

Fruit and vegetable production, distribution, and quality standards are regulated by the Fruit Product Order (FPO), which was established in 1955.

Meat Products Control Orders (1973) (MPO) ensures that the distribution and quality of both processed and unprocessed meat meet the requirements for human consumption.

The Milk and Milk Product Order, 1992 (MMPO) controls the manufacturing and distribution of milk and milk products in order to guarantee that safety and hygienic regulations are followed.

Standards of quality and safety are maintained by the manufacturing and distribution of vegetable oils and commodities being regulated in line with the Vegetable commodities Control Order 1976 and the Solvent Extracted Oils, De-oiled Meal, and Edible Flour Control Order 1967.

## 16.3 Agricultural Produce (Grading and Marketing) Act, 1937 (AGMARK)

AGMARK sets standards for grading and marketing agricultural commodities, assuring consumers of quality. Grades range from special to ordinary based on physical and chemical characteristics. While compliance with AGMARK standards is voluntary, it enhances consumer confidence in the quality of agricultural products.

## 16.4: The Codex Alimentarius

FAO and WHO founded the Codex Alimentarius in 1963 with the purpose of establishing global benchmarks, protocols, and guidelines to guarantee food safety and equitable trade practices. It includes food labeling, additives, contaminants, hygiene, and methods of analysis, among other subjects. Overall Text:

• Nutrition labeling and claims: guidelines and standards for food labeling.

- Specifications and regulations governing the authorized applications of food additives.
- Food contaminant tolerances for particular contaminants.
- Maximum limits on pesticide and veterinary chemical residues.
- Risk assessment procedures: evaluation of the safety of commodities derived from biotechnology.
- Guidelines and principles for food hygiene practices.

**Specific Standards:**

- Meat, fish, and products of the fishing industry.
- Milk and its derivatives.
- Foods intended for specific dietary purposes.
- Produced and unprocessed fruits, vegetables, and beverages.
- Legumes, cereals, lipids, oils, and products derived from them.
- Miscellaneous sustenance items, including mineral water, chocolate, sugar, and honey.

It is imperative that all parties involved in the food industry comprehend and comply with these laws and regulations in order to guarantee the quality and safety of food products that are distributed to consumers around the world.

## 16.5 International Organization for Standardization (ISO)

Global standardization is the responsibility of the International Organization for Standardization (ISO). Representatives from several national standards agencies make up the panel. The organization is based in Geneva, Switzerland, and operates in 164 countries. Founded on February 23, 1947.

One of the first groups to receive general consultative status from the UN Economic and Social Council was ISO. To promote international trade, ISO, the foremost developer of voluntary worldwide standards, makes sure that all nations employ the same vocabulary. It has established more than twenty thousand standards in a variety of fields, such as technology, food safety, manufactured goods, agriculture, and healthcare.

Putting these ideas into practice contributes to the development of dependable, secure, and superior goods and services. They let businesses increase output while cutting down on errors and waste. Facilitating the direct comparison of goods sourced from many nations gives businesses access to new markets and a just contribution to the expansion of global trade. They safeguard customers by verifying that products adhere to fundamental international standards.

**ISO's international standards are developed through six processes by its technical committees (TC) and subcommittees (SC).**

1. Proposal stage 2. Preparation stage

3. Committee phase

4. The investigation phase

5. Approval Stage 6. Publication Stage

ISO's funding sources include organizations that offer expert assistance in technical work or administer specific initiatives.

Contributions from member organizations are determined based on the gross domestic product and trade numbers of each country.

Revenue gained from the sale of standards.

**History of ISO**

ISO originated in 1928 as the International Federation of the National Standardizing Associations (ISA). The United Nations Standards Coordinating Committee (UNSCC) contacted ISA during World War II to propose the creation of a new international standards organization. Delegates from 25 countries gathered in London in October 1946 to collaborate and establish the International Organization for Standardization (ISO). The new organization commenced operations in February 1947.

**Structure of the ISO**

Each member of ISO, a volunteer organization made up of recognized authorities on standards, represents a separate nation. Each year, members get together for a general assembly to discuss ISO's strategic goals. Organizational coordination is handled by a central secretariat located in Geneva. A council made up of twenty entities whose members alternately serve as advisors and provide governance, including setting the Central Secretariat's yearly budget. Over 250 technical committees are under the direction of the Technical Management Board.

**ISO/IEC Joint Technical Committees**

ISO has set up two joint committees with the International Electrotechnical Commission (IEC) to create standards and terminology for electrical and electronic technologies, improving collaboration and knowledge in these disciplines. The ISO/IEC Joint Technical Committee 1 (JTC 1) was established in 1987 with the purpose of developing, maintaining, promoting, and facilitating information technology (IT) standards. ISO/IEC Joint Technical Committee 2 (JTC 2) was established in 2009 to standardize energy efficiency and renewable energy sources.

**Membership in ISO**

ISO has three membership types.

Member bodies are national organizations recognized as the most authoritative standards bodies in their respective countries. These are the sole ISO members with voting privileges.

Correspondent members are countries without their own standards organization. These members are knowledgeable with ISO's activities but do not engage in standard development.

Subscriber members refer to countries with modest economies. They pay discounted membership fees but have access to monitor the progress of standards.

Active participants are referred to as "P" members, whereas passive observers are referred to as "O" members.

**Standardization Process**

It takes a long time for ISO/IEC to issue a standard. The process usually starts with a committee suggesting new work. Here are some shorthand ways to show what status a standard has:

First Work Item, or PWI

NP or NWIP: New Work Item Proposal or New Proposal

AWI: New Work Item Approved

WD: Draft in Progress

CD: Draft by Committee

FCD: Last Draft by the Committee

DIS: Draft of the International Standard

Final Draft of FDIS Standard around the world

A new international standard has been proven (PRF).

"International Standard" is abbreviated as IS. In conclusion, the ISO is an international organization that establishes standards. Members from many national standards organizations make up this group. It was established on February 23, 1947, and its mission is to advance proprietary standards, business, and industry globally. It operates in 164 countries and has its headquarters in Geneva, Switzerland. This organization was among the first to receive general consultative status from the UN Economic and Social Council.

## 16.5.1 ISO 14001:2015: A Guide to Environmental Management Systems

The ISO 14001:2015 standard is a framework that companies all over the world can use to set up effective Environmental Management Systems (EMS). This method helps businesses reduce the damage they do to the environment and do a better job of protecting it overall.

**Key Characteristics of ISO 14001:2015**

Non-Prescriptive: The standard says what needs to be done, but not how it should be done. EMS can be designed in a way that fits the wants and circumstances of each organization.

The PDCA (Plan-Do-Check-Act) Cycle: This loop of iterations is what the standard is all about. Organizations plan their approach, take steps, keep track of progress, and keep making their EMS better.

Focus on the Results: There aren't any set achievement goals, but the focus is on always getting better and being environmentally responsible.

**Building an ISO 14001:2015 Environmental Management System (EMS)**

The standard outlines key components that organizations should address when developing their EMS:

**Plan**

- This is the company's environmental policy. It makes it clear that they want to be good to the earth and always get better.
- It's called "environmental aspects" to look for things, acts, and services that might have an impact on the environment, such as waste production and energy use.
- For legal and other reasons, you have to know and follow all company and environmental rules.
- Plans, goals, and objectives: Setting clear environmental goals, like reducing energy use, making plans for how to reach those goals, and taking action.

**Do**

**Resources, Roles, and Responsibilities:** Assigning clear roles and responsibilities for implementing the EMS within the organization.

**Competence, Training, and Awareness:** Making sure that workers know what they need to know and can do what they need to do to protect the environment.

**Communication:** Establishing clear communication channels regarding environmental policies, procedures, and incidents.

**Documentation:** creating and maintaining documented procedures to ensure consistent implementation of the EMS.

**Operational Control:** Developing procedures to control environmental aspects associated with the organization's operations.

**Emergency Preparedness and Response:** Having plans in place to identify, prepare for, and respond to potential environmental emergencies.

**Check**

**Monitoring and Measurement:** Monitoring key environmental performance indicators (KPIs) to track progress towards objectives and targets.

**Evaluation of Compliance:** Regularly assessing compliance with legal and other environmental requirements.

**Nonconformity, Corrective, and Preventive Action:** Addressing any identified nonconformities (deviations from the EMS) through corrective and preventive actions to prevent recurrence.

**Control of Records:** Maintaining accurate and up-to-date records of environmental data, audits, and actions taken.

**Internal Audits:** conducting periodic internal audits to assess the effectiveness of the EMS and identify areas for improvement.

**Act**

**Management Review:** Senior management regularly reviews the EMS performance, objectives, and targets, making necessary adjustments to ensure continuous improvement.

**ISO 14001 Audit (Optional):** Organizations can undergo an external audit by a certified body to demonstrate conformity with the ISO 14001:2015 standard (not mandatory for certification).

**Benefits of Implementing ISO 14001:2015**

**Reduced Environmental Impact:** Organizations can minimize their environmental footprint through better resource management and pollution prevention.

**Enhanced Compliance:** A structured EMS helps ensure compliance with environmental regulations.

**Cost Savings:** Costs can be cut by cutting down on trash and energy use and making operations more efficient.

**Improved Brand Reputation:** Demonstrating environmental responsibility can enhance brand image and customer trust.

**Competitive Advantage:** A strong EMS can give organizations a competitive edge in markets that prioritize sustainability.

Finally, ISO 14001:2015 gives businesses a useful structure for building a strong environmental management system. Companies can reduce their damage to the environment, follow the rules, and reach their environmental sustainability goals by using this strategy.

## *Review Questions:*

1. What is the objective of the Prevention of Food Adulteration Act, 1954?
2. Discuss the main provisions of the Essential Commodities Act, 1955, and their relevance to food regulation.
3. Explain the significance of AGMARK in agricultural produce marketing.
4. What is the purpose of the Codex Alimentarius, and how does it contribute to global food safety?
5. Provide examples of control orders under the Essential Commodities Act and their implications for food quality.
6. How does the Codex Alimentarius ensure fair trade practices in the food industry?
7. Discuss the role of food labeling standards in consumer protection.
8. Why is compliance with AGMARK standards beneficial for agricultural producers?
9. What are the key components of the Codex Alimentarius?
10. How do specific standards under the Codex Alimentarius address the quality and safety of food products?
11. What is the purpose of the Prevention of Food Adulteration Act, 1954, and how does it contribute to food safety?
12. Explain the Essential Commodities Act, 1955, and its impact on the production, trade, and circulation of essential goods.
13. Discuss the role of the Agricultural Produce (Grading and Marketing) Act, 1937 (AGMARK) in assuring the quality of agricultural products.

14. How does the Codex Alimentarius contribute to global food safety and fair trade practices?
15. Describe the key components of the International Organization for Standardization (ISO) and its role in standardization worldwide.
16. Discuss the significance of ISO 14001:2015 in establishing effective Environmental Management Systems (EMS).
17. How do the Fruit Product Order, 1955 (FPO), and Meat Products Control Orders of 1973 contribute to food quality and safety?
18. What are the benefits of implementing ISO 14001:2015 for businesses?
19. Discuss the process of standardization in ISO and its impact on international trade.
20. How does the Milk and Milk Product Order, 1992 (MMPO), ensure hygiene and safety standards in the production and distribution of milk and milk products?

**Learning Activity:** Organize a mock regulatory compliance workshop where students simulate the process of assessing food products for compliance with various food laws and regulations, including the Prevention of Food Adulteration Act, Essential Commodities Act, AGMARK standards, and Codex Alimentarius guidelines. Provide case studies and scenarios for students to analyze and discuss potential regulatory issues and solutions.

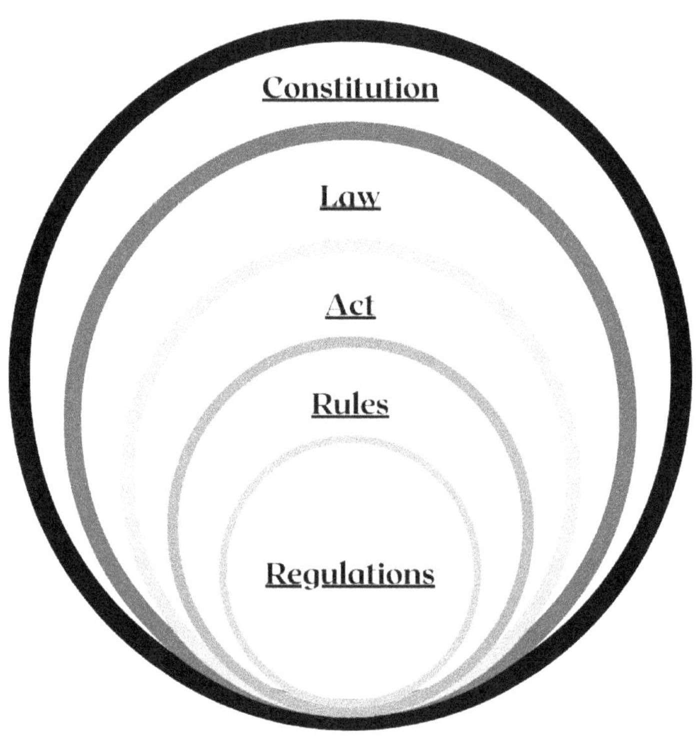


Law Act

# CHAPTER XVII

# Total Quality Management (TQM)

*"Continuous improvement isn't an option—it's the path to lasting excellence."*

This chapter offers an in-depth exploration of Total Quality Management (TQM), a potent management philosophy emphasizing continuous improvement throughout all organizational facets. Originating from W. Edwards Deming's vision in post-World War II Japan, TQM has evolved from a reconstruction strategy into a widely embraced approach for achieving superior product or service quality, fostering robust employee engagement, and nurturing enduring customer relationships.

Total Quality Management (TQM) is a management methodology that focuses on ensuring high quality standards. It involves the active involvement of all individuals within an organization and is designed to achieve long-term success by prioritizing customer happiness and benefiting all stakeholders, including society.

Total Quality Management (TQM) is a systematic approach that utilizes quantitative methodologies and human resources to enhance all organizational operations and surpass consumer requirements, both presently and in the long term. It combines core management practices, ongoing improvement initiatives, and technical tools into a structured strategy.

TQM aims to deliver superior products and services to customers, boost efficiency, reduce expenses, improve competitive standing in the market, attain organizational goals of profitability and expansion, and establish a gratifying work atmosphere for employees.

## 17.1 The Pillars of TQM: Core Concepts

TQM is built upon several foundational principles:

**Customer Focus**: Prioritizing understanding and exceeding customer needs in all operations.

**Continuous Improvement**: Embracing systematic and ongoing enhancement of quality.

**Employee Empowerment**: Equipping all employees to actively contribute to quality improvement.

**Quality Assurance**: Implementing robust tools and techniques to establish and maintain high-quality standards.

**Management Commitment**: Ensuring leadership dedication to fostering a culture obsessed with quality.

## 17.2 Principles of TQM

A set of fundamental principles serves as the foundation for TQM, including:

1. Management Takes the Lead: Top leadership carries primary responsibility for ensuring product quality.
2. The Customer Defines Quality: Quality is measured against standards defined by the customer.
3. Quality by Design: Processes and methods are meticulously designed to achieve consistent quality.
4. Everyone Owns Quality: Every employee shares accountability for product quality.
5. Do It Right the First Time: Focus on preventing defects rather than fixing them later.
6. Continuous Monitoring and Improvement: Proactive monitoring to identify and address quality issues promptly.
7. The Journey Never Ends: The pursuit of continuous improvement is an ongoing commitment.

8. Partnerships for Quality: Extending TQM practices to suppliers to guarantee high-quality inputs.

**"Let's explore the foundational pillars that uphold total quality management":**
1. Customer-Focused Organization
2. Leadership
3. Involvement of people
4. Process Approach
5. A System Approach to Management
6. Continual Improvement
7. A Factual Approach to Decision Making
8. Mutually Beneficial Supplier Relationships"

## 17.3 Frameworks for Implementing TQM

Several models and frameworks provide a roadmap for implementing TQM, including:

1. Deming Prize for Applications
2. Malcolm Baldrige Criteria for High-Quality Work
3. The European Foundation for Quality Management (EFQM) offers ISO Quality Management Standards.Deming Award for Uses
4. Malcolm Baldrige Standards for Excellent Work
5. The European Foundation for Quality Management (EFQM) offers ISO Quality Management Standards.

**Steps to TQM Implementation**

- Vision First: Define clear organizational goals and objectives to ensure actions align with the overall mission.
- Defining Success: Identify critical success factors (CSFs) and establish metrics to measure progress.

- Engaging Everyone: Solicit employee input and participation in quality improvement initiatives.
- Crafting a Roadmap: Develop actionable plans to address identified areas for improvement.
- Taking Action: Systematically implement solutions to address problems and seize opportunities for enhancement.
- Measuring Progress: Assess the effectiveness of improvement efforts through data analysis.
- Learning from Results: Make data-driven changes based on evaluation outcomes to sustain progress.
- Standardizing Success: Formalize successful practices for ongoing improvement.
- Ensuring Sustainability: Monitor and reinforce initiatives to guarantee long-term success.

**Establishing a TQM System: A Step-by-Step Guide**

1. Vision, Mission, and Values: Align organizational objectives with operational strategies.
2. Critical Success Factors: Identify key performance indicators to track progress.
3. Metrics and Measurement: Establish mechanisms to monitor and assess CSF data.
4. Knowing Your Customers: Identify and prioritize the needs of various customer segments.
5. The Voice of the Customer: Actively seek input from customers to inform improvement efforts.
6. Creating a Feedback Tool: Develop customized surveys to gather relevant customer feedback.
7. Listening to All Customers: Conduct structured surveys to assess customer satisfaction and perception across different segments.
8. Turning Feedback into Action: Craft actionable plans based on customer feedback and identify improvement areas.
9. The Feedback Loop Continues: Periodically reassess customer satisfaction to gauge the effectiveness of improvement

initiatives.

10. Monitoring Performance: Continuously monitor performance metrics to ensure sustained progress.
11. Customer Satisfaction: A Marketing Tool: Leverage positive outcomes to enhance brand reputation and market presence.
12. Technology for Improvement: Utilize technology to support targeted improvements and streamline processes.


## *Review Questions*


1. State the purpose of Total Quality Management (TQM).
2. How is quality defined in different contexts?
3. How has the concept of quality evolved since the Industrial Revolution?
4. What are some modern approaches to quality management?
5. How does quality contribute to competitiveness and success?
6. Discuss the role of stakeholders in quality management. Provide examples.
7. Analyze the eight principles of Total Quality Management (TQM) and their importance in achieving long-term success through customer satisfaction.
8. Define Total Quality Management (TQM) and explain its origin.
9. Discuss the role of W. Edwards Deming in the evolution of TQM.
10. What are the core concepts or pillars of TQM? Explain each.
11. List and explain the fundamental principles that serve as the foundation for TQM.
12. How does TQM approach the concept of 'Quality by Design'?
13. Discuss the importance of 'Continuous Monitoring and Improvement' in TQM.
14. What are the key steps to implementing TQM in an organization?
15. Discuss the role of 'Customer Satisfaction' as a marketing tool in TQM.

16. How does TQM utilize technology for improvement and process streamlining?

Discuss the various frameworks for implementing TQM, including the Deming Prize for Applications, Malcolm Baldrige Criteria for High-Quality Work, and ISO Quality Management Standards from the European Foundation for Quality Management (EFQM).

**Learning Activity:** Conduct a TQM case study analysis where students examine real-life examples of organizations that have successfully implemented TQM principles. Students can identify key TQM concepts and practices applied by these organizations and evaluate their effectiveness in improving quality, enhancing customer satisfaction, and achieving business success.

TQM

# CHAPTER XVIII

# The Significance of Hygiene in Food Safety

*""Clean hands and clean practices build a foundation for safe food and healthy lives."*"

There is widespread concern regarding food safety, and all individuals involved in handling food have a moral obligation to ensure its safety and healthiness. Ensuring the safety, taste, and quality of food throughout the whole supply chain is crucial. Good hygiene practices (GHPs) and good production procedures (GMPs) can be beneficial in this regard.

"Hygiene" encompasses all practices and behaviors that promote health and prevent illness, particularly those related to cleanliness. Food hygiene refers to the necessary conditions and procedures to ensure the safety and suitability of food at all times.

Our food should possess high quality in terms of appearance, aroma, flavor, texture, nutritional content, purity, cost, consistency, and safety. Food safety ensures that while preparing and consuming food as intended, you can be confident that it is safe for consumption and will not cause harm.

Opt for food that is clean, appropriately ripe, and free of pollutants to ensure food safety. Fruits and vegetables from the farm will deteriorate in quality and nutritional content if stored in a dry area instead of the refrigerator.

## 18.1 Equipment Hygiene

Cleaning schedules must be carefully organized and adhered to in order to ensure that the premises, equipment, furnishings, fittings, and fixtures are cleaned thoroughly. All surfaces must be clean and free from dust, grime, grease, stains, cobwebs, or any other undesirable substances.

Choose suitable cleaning techniques including water and a cleaning solution based on the type of dirt or soil that needs to be eliminated. It is essential to uphold a thorough cleaning and sanitation regimen that outlines the equipment to be cleaned, cleaning schedule, cleaning methods, and the precise tools and supplies required for cleaning.

The three fundamental phases in all cleaning methods are: Washing (with detergent and a scourer), Rinsing (with clean water), and Sanitizing (using hot water or chemicals). Dishes that have been cleaned should be allowed to air-dry and kept properly to prevent contamination. Documentation of cleaning with sanitizers is necessary due to the toxicity of some sanitizers and the need to rinse off any residue. Disconnect electrical equipment before cleaning and sanitizing.

## 18.2 The 7 C's of Food Hygiene

The following considerations should be made in order to make food safe and avoid contaminating, growing, and surviving microbes in it:

**Check**: Examine all products for quality before making a purchase and only buy from recognized retailers. Select healthy food when it is perfectly ripe. No pollutants found. When frozen at the appropriate temperature. When packaging items, check the 'best before date' and confirm that the packaging is intact.

**Clean**: Clean all packages, tins, bottles, etc., before placing them in the designated storage place. Select and prepare leafy vegetables by discarding any damaged leaves, inedible stems, and roots. Thoroughly clean entire fruits, vegetables, and eggs before keeping by washing and draining/drying them.

**Cover**: When storing food or preparing and serving it, keep it covered. In the dry food store, keep stable foods in hygienic, dry, covered containers. If lids are not available, cover the container with aluminum foil or cling film. Covering food in the refrigerator helps keep it from getting contaminated, drying out, or absorbing smells.

**Cross Contamination Avoid**: Hand washing is essential before handling food. Don't combine cooked and raw ingredients. Use different cutting boards and knives for prepared and raw food. Store uncooked food underneath cooked food.

**Cook**: Cooking effectively eradicates dangerous microbes. Improves digestibility. Improves taste, flavor, and aroma. Improves appearance and prevents enzymatic browning. Extends the shelf life. Thaw frozen food before cooking it. Make sure that any remaining food is thoroughly cooked before consuming. Stir the food in the microwave oven to promote even cooking/heating.

**Cool/Chill**: If food is going to be given later and is perishable or could be dangerous, cool it within 1 ½ hours. Use small bowls or an ice/water bath to cool food. To cool faster, cool in small amounts. Within 1 ½ to 2 hours, put food in the fridge or freezer.

**Consume**: Keep the area where you serve food clean. Clean the plates and spoons. As much as possible, eat food that has just been made. Keep hot food above 65℃ and things that go bad quickly out of the danger zone. After the meal, wash the dishes well with water.

## Review Questions

1. What are Good Hygienic Practices (GHPs) and Good Manufacturing Practices (GMPs)?
2. What is the difference between "Hygiene" and "Food Hygiene"?
3. What are the key factors that determine the quality of the food we eat?
4. What does the term "food safety" mean?
5. Why is it important to select wholesome food at the right stage of maturity?
6. What are the three basic steps of all cleaning methods?
7. What are the 7 C's of Food Hygiene and what does each one mean?

8. Why is it important to keep raw and cooked food apart?
9. What are the benefits of proper cooking?
10. Why is it important to cool food within 1 ½ to 2 hrs if it is perishable/potentially hazardous and is to be served later?

**Learning Activity:** Conduct a hygiene audit of a local food processing facility or restaurant, where students assess adherence to hygiene practices based on the 7 C's framework. Students can identify areas of improvement and develop recommendations to enhance hygiene standards and prevent food safety risks.

# Personal Hygiene

# CHAPTER XIX

# Food Adulteration

*""Compromising quality for profit is not just deception—it's a betrayal of trust."*

*"He who does not prevent a crime when he can, encourages it." — Seneca"*

Its purpose is to reduce the quality of food by introducing undesirable substances or removing beneficial ones. The term for this is food adulteration. In other words, adulteration refers to the deliberate addition of an additional substance, often one that is detrimental or of inferior quality, to food or drink with the intention of increasing profits at the expense of consumers.

In accordance with the Federal Food, Drug, and Cosmetic (FD&C) Act of 1938, the following constitutes "adulterated" food:

It contains or contains a "poisonous or deleterious substance" that may be hazardous to your health.

Food is deemed adulterated when it contains any hazardous substances other than those specified, such as food additives or pesticide residues.

Its container is composed of a hazardous or noxious material that may expose its contents to health risks, or it contains or has been exposed to a hazardous pesticide chemical residue.

Food also meets the definition of adulteration if:

1. It is, possesses, or comprises a hazardous food additive.
2. It is, carries, or comprises a novel animal drug that is hazardous. It contains, carries, or is composed of a hazardous color additive.
3. It is otherwise unsuitable for human consumption or comprises "any putrid, decomposed, or filthy substance," either in its entirety or in part.

4. The item in question has been handled, packaged, or prepared in an unhygienic environment (insect, rodent, or avian infestation), which may have resulted in its contamination with waste or toxicity to human health.

As an illustration, adulterated products include apple cider tainted with E. coli O157:H7 and Brie cheese tainted with Listeria monocytogenes.

## 19.1 Types of Food Adulteration

Foreign stuff and dirt refer to any unwanted things present in meals. This refers to contaminants such as stones, sand, metal, and plastic, as well as undesired elements found in the original plant material (e.g., stems and pits in pitted olives or shell fragments in canned oysters), along with decay, excrement, insect and rodent fragments, and decomposition.

Economic adulteration is the act of intentionally leaving out a valuable component from a product or replacing it with another material. For instance, olive oil mixed with tea tree oil, fresh fruit with added food coloring to hide imperfections, or any product altered to increase its quantity or weight, reduce its quality or strength, or give the false impression of being more significant or valuable than it actually is. For example, scallops that have been enhanced with water to boost their weight.

Adulteration and microbial contamination: Pathogens in food may or may not suggest adulteration. Pathogens typically contaminate ready-to-eat foods. For example, ready-to-eat meat or poultry goods like luncheon meats or fresh fruits and vegetables could be contaminated with Salmonella.

The federal Food and Drug Administration forbids the interstate shipment of contaminated foods, pharmaceuticals, and cosmetics as mandated by the Food, Drug, and Cosmetic Administration.

## *Review Questions*

1. What is food adulteration?
2. What are the criteria for a food to be considered "adulterated" according to the Federal Food, Drug, and Cosmetic (FD&C) Act (1938)?
3. What are some examples of "poisonous or deleterious substances" that may render food injurious to health?
4. What is the difference between a food additive and a color additive?
5. What are some examples of "filth and foreign matter" in food?
6. What is economic adulteration? Provide an example.
7. How does microbiological contamination lead to food adulteration?
8. What are some examples of pathogens that can render food adulterated?
9. What is the role of the federal Food and Drug Administration in preventing food adulteration?
10. Why is it important to prevent food adulteration?

**Learning Activity:** Conduct a simulated food adulteration investigation, where students are presented with different food samples and tasked with identifying potential adulterants using chemical, physical, and microbiological testing methods. Students can analyze results and propose corrective actions to address detected adulteration issues.

Substitution
Dilution
Concealment
Food Fraud
Counterfeiting
Mislabeling
Unapproved Enhancements
Grey Market

Food Fraud

# Appendix A: Glossary Of Fqm Key Terms

1. **Acceptance Testing**: Evaluating a food product based on consumer preferences and determining its degree of liking.
2. **Advanced Product Quality Planning (APQP)**: A structured process for ensuring a product's design integrity throughout manufacturing (think: blueprint for quality).
3. **Affective Sensory Analysis**: Involves assessing consumer preferences and liking for food products through methods like preference testing and acceptance testing.
4. **Agricultural Produce (Grading and Marketing) Act, 1937 (AGMARK)**: Provides standards for grading and marketing agricultural commodities to ensure consumer confidence in the quality of agricultural products.
5. **Appraisal Costs:** Appraisal costs are the expenses associated with evaluating and inspecting food products to ensure they meet quality standards. This includes testing, inspections, and other quality assurance activities.
6. **Artificial Intelligence (AI) in Food Quality Management**: The application of AI involves using algorithms to analyze data and make intelligent decisions in various aspects of food quality management.
7. **Artificial Intelligence (AI)**: Involves the use of computer algorithms to analyze data, make decisions, and perform tasks, transforming various aspects of food quality management.
8. **Biosensors**: Miniature analytical devices that combine biological components with electronic systems, used for rapid and accurate detection of foodborne pathogens.
9. **Calibration**: The process of configuring an instrument to provide a result for a sample within an acceptable range by comparing the measurements of two different systems.
10. **Change Management:** A system for controlling changes to processes and documents, ensuring transparency and

traceability.

11. **Codex Alimentarius**: "A collection of internationally recognized standards, guidelines, and recommendations pertaining to food safety and quality, developed by the Codex Alimentarius Commission".

12. **Codex Alimentarius**: "The World Health Organization (WHO) and the Food and Agriculture Organization (FAO) set up this set of international food standards and codes of behavior to protect consumer health and encourage fair trade in food".

13. **Competitive Advantage:** Achieving a market edge through superior food quality and safety, leading to increased customer satisfaction and brand loyalty.

14. **Complaint Management:** The process for handling customer complaints, analyzing their cause, and taking corrective action (think: addressing customer concerns).

15. **Consumer Satisfaction:** Consumer satisfaction reflects how pleased customers are with a food product. It considers their overall experience, including their perceptions, preferences, and how the food measures up to their expectations.

16. **Contaminants in Foods:** Substances that may pose health risks when present in food products, including heavy metals, pesticides, and microbial pathogens.

17. **Control Charts:** A type of graph used in quality control processes to study how a process changes over time. It helps in identifying any variations in the process that may affect the quality of the output.

18. **Corrective Action (CA):** Steps taken to address identified problems in the production process (think: fixing what went wrong).

19. **Corrective Action Management (CAPA):** A structured approach to identifying the root cause of problems, implementing corrective actions, and preventing future occurrences (think: fixing what went wrong and preventing it from happening again).

20. **Cost of Poor Quality:** The cost of poor quality refers to the

financial burden caused by defects, errors, and inefficiencies in food production and delivery. This includes expenses related to reworking products, recalls, and dealing with customer complaints.

21. **Critical Control Points (CCPs)**: "Specific stages in the food production process where control measures can be applied to prevent, eliminate, or reduce food safety hazards to acceptable levels".

22. **Descriptive Sensory Analysis**: Involves the objective description and quantification of sensory attributes of food products by trained panelists.

23. **Document Control and Management:** Tracking, maintaining versions of, and storing documents to ensure their accuracy and integrity (think: keeping track of important paperwork).

24. **Employee Involvement**: Actively engaging employees in quality initiatives, leading to improved morale, problem-solving, and productivity.

25. **Enterprise Quality Management Software (EQMS):** Software that streamlines quality management across the entire organization (think: all-in-one quality management toolkit).

26. **Essential Commodities Act, 1955**: Legislation aimed at regulating the manufacture, commerce, and distribution of essential commodities, including food products.

27. **Extrinsic Factors:** Extrinsic factors are external conditions that can affect the quality and safety of food. This includes how it's handled, stored, processed, packaged, and transported.

28. **Failure Costs:** Failure costs are the financial penalties incurred due to defects and quality failures in food products. This includes the cost of throwing away unusable food (scrap), reworking products, handling warranty claims, and dealing with customer returns.

29. **Food Additives**: Substances added to food products to preserve flavor, enhance texture, or prolong shelf life, subject to regulatory approval and safety standards.

30. **Food Fraud**: "Food items that are changed, substituted, or lied

about on purpose to make money, putting consumers' health and safety at risk".

31. **Food Hygiene**: Practices and procedures aimed at preventing foodborne illnesses, including proper handling, storage, and preparation of food products.

32. **Food Inspection**: Thorough examination and evaluation of food products to ensure compliance with quality and safety standards before distribution and consumption.

33. **Food Labelling**: Providing information on food packaging about ingredients, nutritional content, and allergens to inform consumers and ensure transparency.

34. **Food Quality Assurance Programs**: Systematic approaches designed to mitigate risks and ensure the consistent production of safe, high-quality food products.

35. **Food Quality Management Systems:** A structured framework for ensuring food safety and consistently meeting quality standards throughout the food supply chain, from farm to fork.

36. **Food Quality Parameters**: Measurable characteristics used to assess the quality of food products, including sensory attributes, nutritional content, and safety criteria.

37. **Food Quality Regulation:** Government regulations that set quality standards for food products, such as composition, labeling, and safety specifications.

38. **Food quality**: Food quality refers to the aspects of food quality that meet customer standards. This includes characteristics like size, form, color, gloss, and consistency on the outside, as well as chemical, physical, and microbial traits on the inside, as well as texture and flavor on the outside. Federal grade standards for eggs are an example of this. Food quality also looks at how the product can be tracked back to its original sources, like the companies that provided the ingredients and packing, in case a recall is needed. It also addresses labeling issues so that the accuracy of ingredient and nutrition information can be checked.

39. **Food Safety and Standards Authority of India (FSSAI):** "The

Indian regulatory body responsible for ensuring food safety and regulating food imports, manufacturing, storage, distribution, and sale in India".

40. **Food Safety Management System (FSMS)**: Policies, procedures, and practices implemented to ensure the safety of food products throughout the supply chain, from production to consumption.

41. **Food Safety Plans (FSVP)**: Outline preventive controls to ensure the safety of food products, including measures to identify and mitigate potential hazards.

42. **Food Safety Plans**: A written plan that demonstrates how a facility will control food safety hazards to ensure that the food is safe for consumption.

43. **Food Safety Regulation**: Government regulations designed to protect consumers from foodborne illnesses by establishing safety standards for food production, processing, and distribution.

44. **Food Safety**: Measures taken to ensure that food products are free from contamination and pathogens, safeguarding consumer health.

45. **Foodborne Illness**: Diseases caused by consuming contaminated food or beverages, resulting from the ingestion of pathogens, toxins, or chemical contaminants.

46. **Foodborne Pathogens**: Microorganisms, including bacteria, viruses, and parasites, that can cause illness when consumed in contaminated food products.

47. **Gauge Management**: Tracking and reporting the accuracy of measuring instruments to ensure they provide reliable data (think: making sure measuring tools are accurate).

48. **Goal Setting**: Establishing specific, measurable objectives for food quality improvement to guide organizational efforts and monitor progress.

49. **Good Agricultural Practices (GAP)**: Principles applied in on-farm production and post-production processes to ensure the safety and quality of agricultural products.

50. **Good Manufacturing Practices (GMP)**: The set of rules and

procedures that make sure that safe, high-quality food items are always made, with a focus on cleanliness, hygiene, and quality control.

51. **HACCP Plan**: A planned method for finding and managing risks in food production, which makes sure that food is safe and that rules are followed.

52. **Hazard Analysis and Critical Control Points (HACCP)**: A planned, proactive approach to food safety that looks at physical, chemical, and biological risks as a way to stop them from happening instead of inspecting the finished product.

53. **International Organization for Standardization (ISO) Standards**: Globally recognized guidelines for quality management and assurance in various industries (think: quality benchmarks).

54. **Intrinsic Factors**: Intrinsic factors are the built-in properties of a food, like its makeup, structure, and chemical composition. These qualities significantly influence the food's safety and overall quality.

55. **ISO 22000**: A set of international standards for food safety management systems, providing a framework for organizations to implement HACCP principles and achieve consistent food safety.

56. **Layered Process Audit (LPA)**: A method for conducting internal audits to assess compliance with quality standards (think: quality check-ups).

57. **Materials Management Operations Guidelines (MMOG)**: Best practices for supply chain management, helping organizations assess and improve their processes (think: optimizing how materials are sourced and managed).

58. **Meat Products Control Orders, 1973 (MPO)**: Regulates the manufacturing, quality, and distribution of raw and processed meat products to ensure safety and compliance with standards.

59. **New Product Introduction (NPI)**: Software that facilitates the development and launch of new products while minimizing costs and maximizing quality (think: bringing new products to

market faster and better).

60. **Nonconformance Report (NCR):** A document recording a quality issue, the corrective action taken, and steps to prevent recurrence (think: documenting problems and solutions).

61. **Non-Destructive Techniques:** Methods for evaluating food quality without altering the product, preserving its integrity for further analysis or consumption.

62. **Novel Food Technologies:** Emerging technologies used in food production, processing, and preservation, requiring careful evaluation to ensure safety and consumer acceptance.

63. **Online Food Sales:** The growing trend of purchasing food products through online platforms, which requires robust food safety measures throughout the online supply chain.

64. **Pesticide and Veterinary Chemical Residues in Foods:** Maximum residue limits set for pesticides and veterinary chemicals in foods to ensure consumer safety and compliance with regulations.

65. **Preference Testing:** Assessing consumer preferences for food products to determine which attributes are preferred and which are disliked.

66. **Pre-Harvest Handling and Storage Practices:** Procedures employed to maintain the quality of agricultural produce before harvest, including field sanitation, optimal harvesting time, and immediate cooling.

67. **Pre-Requisite Programs (PRPs):** Basic conditions and actions needed to keep the environment clean along the food chain so that safe goods can be made, handled, and distributed, as well as safe food for people to eat.

68. **Prevention Costs:** "Prevention costs are the investments made to avoid quality issues in food production. This can involve training employees, implementing quality control systems, and performing preventive maintenance on equipment".

69. **Prevention of Food Adulteration Act, 1954 (PFA):** Legislation aimed at preventing the adulteration of food products, including regulations on food standards, sampling procedures, and

penalties for non-compliance.

70. **Preventive Controls**: Measures implemented to prevent potential hazards in food production, including sanitation procedures, employee training, and hazard analysis.

71. **Process Adherence**: Following established procedures to achieve consistent quality (think: sticking to the quality playbook).

72. **Process Audit**: Evaluating production processes to identify areas for improvement (think: quality checkup for production lines).

73. **Production Part Approval Process (PPAP)**: A system in the automotive industry that ensures suppliers consistently produce high-quality products (think: guaranteeing quality from suppliers).

74. **Quality Assurance**: Systematic processes and procedures to ensure that food products meet specified quality standards and customer expectations.

75. **Quality Control (QC)**: QC was created to make sure that quality standards are met. It checks every step of the manufacturing process. The company often uses methods like operational auditing and inspection to make sure that the given product or service meets its goals. QC is all about the result of the process.

76. **Quality improvement**: It is an organizational practice that sets up ways to evaluate and improve processes based on their adaptability, effectiveness, and speed, among other things. This can be done either by making big changes that can be seen or by making small improvements over time.

77. **Quality Leadership**: Involves setting the tone for a culture of quality within an organization and providing direction and support to ensure adherence to quality standards.

78. **Quality Management Standards**: Guidelines for ensuring consistent product quality (think: quality benchmarks).

79. **Quality Management System (QMS)**: A set of policies and procedures designed to achieve operational excellence and customer satisfaction (think: roadmap for achieving quality).

80. **Quality Management**: There are four main parts of quality

management: planning for quality, ensuring quality, controlling quality, and improving quality. Quality management also looks at the ways that products and services are made to be of high quality. To make sure that the quality of both processes and goods is always the same, quality management uses control and quality assurance. Quality depends on what the customer wants and is willing to pay for. As a result, quality can be thought of as how well a product does what it's supposed to do, or how fit it is for its intended use.

81. **Quality Planning:** Organizations use quality planning to "make the products, systems, and processes that are needed to meet or exceed customer expectations." Identifying the customer, figuring out what they need, and making the tools (systems, methods, etc.) they need to get those things done are all part of this.

82. **Quality Process Compliance:** Meeting regulatory requirements for product quality (think: following the quality rules).

83. **Regulatory Compliance:** Adherence to laws, regulations, and standards governing food production, processing, labeling, and distribution to ensure consumer protection and public health.

84. **Risk Assessment:** Identifying potential hazards in food products and evaluating the likelihood and severity of adverse effects on consumer health.

85. **Risk Management:** Identifying potential problems and taking steps to prevent them (think: anticipating and mitigating quality risks).

86. **Safe Quality Food (SQF):** A food safety and quality certification program recognized by retailers and food manufacturers globally, demonstrating a commitment to rigorous food safety standards.

87. **Sampling Techniques:** Methods used to select a subset of individuals from a statistical population to estimate characteristics of the whole population.

88. **Sensory Attributes:** Sensory attributes are the qualities we experience through our senses: sight (appearance), smell

(aroma), taste (flavor), touch (texture), and even mouthfeel. These all contribute to how much we enjoy food.

89. **Sensory Evaluation**: The scientific discipline that uses human senses to evaluate the sensory characteristics of food products.

90. **Shelf Life**: The duration during which a food product remains safe and retains its quality characteristics under specified storage conditions.

91. **Six Sigma**: A data-driven methodology for process improvement, aiming to minimize defects and maximize efficiency (think: achieving near-perfect quality).

92. **Solvent Extracted Oils, De-oiled Meal, and Edible Flour Control Order 1967**: "This order regulates the manufacture and distribution of solvent extracted oils, de-oiled meals, edible flours, and hydrogenated vegetable oils to ensure compliance with quality standards".

93. **Standards**: Established criteria or specifications used to define the quality attributes of food products, ensuring consistency and conformity to desired benchmarks.

94. **Statistical Process Control (SPC) Techniques**: "Involve using statistical methods to monitor and control processes to ensure consistency and quality in food production".

95. **Statistical Process Control (SPC)**: Using statistical methods to monitor and control the production process, identifying variations and ensuring consistency in product quality.

96. **Taste Testing**: Evaluating food products based on their flavor characteristics and sensory appeal to determine consumer preferences.

97. **Total Quality Management (TQM)**: A company-wide approach to achieving quality at every stage of a product's lifecycle (think: quality from start to finish).

98. **Traceability**: "Refers to the ability to track a food product through all stages of production, processing, and distribution, crucial for food safety and quality control".

99. **Training Compliance Management**: Tracking employee training to ensure they have the skills and knowledge necessary

for quality production (think: making sure workers have the quality know-how).

100. **U.S. Food and Drug Administration (FDA):** "The US government body in charge of keeping people healthy by making sure that drugs, biological products, medical devices, and our food supply are safe, effective, and secure".

101. **Validation:** The process of checking if something satisfies a certain criterion. In the context of quality control, it often refers to the process of checking if a system meets the system requirements.

102. **Vegetable Products Control Order 1976:** "This order regulates the manufacturing and distribution of vegetable products to ensure compliance with quality standards and safety requirements".

103. **Blockchain in Food Traceability:** The use of blockchain technology to create transparent and secure records of food products' journey from farm to table, enhancing traceability and accountability in the food supply chain.

104. **Nutritional Profiling:** The process of analyzing the nutritional content of food products, including macronutrients and micronutrients, to ensure they meet health and dietary standards.

105. **Sustainable Food Production Practices:** Methods and strategies aimed at reducing the environmental impact of food production, including efficient resource use, waste reduction, and organic farming practices.

106. **Food Packaging Innovations:** The development and application of new packaging materials and technologies to enhance food preservation, reduce waste, and improve consumer convenience.

# Appendix B: Online Resources Downloads- Powerpoint

**PPT Prepared By**
**Scan QR Code to download**
**Title of PowerPoint Presentation**
**PPT Link to Download**
R Biakthanchami

Dimension of Product

https://drive.google.com/
open?id=1KFasYKTW1IoP1FYEenklxD9gt7ub_hcv
Ramengmawii

## Cost of Quality

https://drive.google.com/
open?id=1YxCJWvUMfco3rdKdMU68K6r5DKMkixR8

Stephen H Lalbiaksanga

## Quality Statement - Vision, Mission & Quality policy

https://drive.google.com/
open?id=1n6zyFyaBgisf1Sy7y99jjfodCf7N1ZaW

Jacob Lalrinfela Tlau

Juran Corsby 14 steps

https://drive.google.com/
open?id=1W0jeaO0bjOh-pwb7hh1aDgNYV9658CmJ
Lalrengpuia

Japanese 5s principles

https://drive.google.com/
open?id=1bTpVoiWwbwFBY6AtLrfundYc2HBN2Om8
R Lalrinkima

TQM Frameworks &benifits

https://drive.google.com/
open?id=1qvLEXRtyvnZ0E3sVkxQy17xh-ZoPXRAn
Rohluzuala Chawngthu

Contribution of Edward Deming

https://drive.google.com/
open?id=17YPApsHZpsvysThCSXBoOwujjv70sFeC
Lalremdika

Ishikawa Contribution

https://drive.google.com/
open?id=1g6t0imDnNdTnF4FCxV03GeVt5iHBKlRr

Lalremsangi

Goal and importance of cost of quality

https://drive.google.com/
open?id=1WL9dw1jGcZK58kGL2g4eiqqUMa4bh2--
Pc Lalhmahruaia

Customer focus and customer perception

https://drive.google.com/
open?id=1nAV9fTJAVLOHmdFH5JLqiK4uiyRefZDf
Fraser Chuausangliana

Taguchi Contributions

https://drive.google.com/
open?id=1TChUVVAaTNJzfbfsk-ISbepfAgW77Gcv
H Lalzawnchhuahi

Understanding Quality:Vision,Mission,and Policy Statements

https://drive.google.com/
open?id=1DL2rfLZ75vSuOXaBOK4UmHYnK-7qU9vV
F Lalropuii

Benefits and obstacles of total quality Management

https://drive.google.com/
open?id=1ShsxnBqEAEvWNgnBiQ_AlZ7paVNjXC9d
Lalremtluangi Sailo

Taguchi techniques in quality management

https://drive.google.com/
open?id=1sb7iltY1LYnGVpiZijsmwoe42e4VbErV
N Gabriel Remlalnghaka

Understanding Capital Requirements in Resort Business

https://drive.google.com/
open?id=1hk43RmRoQPH6OrciVqb7KKR_E7jWOq9n
Lalchhanchhuaha

Cost of quality: Understanding the cost associated with quality management

https://drive.google.com/
open?id=1QVmmk9U66WlUBOG64uoVvq3ltST3FD-r
Lalchhanhima

Contribution of Deming to Quality Management

https://drive.google.com/
open?id=1l8Z2v_9v0T1aQ9wc2R_qaWpOlkOyAutG
Lallawmsangi

contribution of feignbaum to quality management

https://drive.google.com/
open?id=10U4rR2hiI_l34CnxuuqvhEh8aoo1pw_1
Malsawmdawngliani

Introduction to Quality Circles

https://drive.google.com/
open?id=1vWZ0_1Gi5iKy5XDrcSa9dUmNVnrDooQ8

## C.Zothanpuia

Introduction to TQM Framework

https://drive.google.com/
open?id=1WYmFRO9h2NOYtHTTe4fLvz8AynETni8k

## Ismael Lalduhsaka

Customer Focus in Quality Management

https://drive.google.com/
open?id=1MOO3SArmECeiUK9XHr9WZn1e8TcbKZPW
Lalpekhlua

Ishikawa's contribution to Quality Management

https://drive.google.com/
open?id=1DJqpnf-traQsLd3kRoa2MtasepA7YJ9F
Trinyard R Marak

QMS(Cost of quality &its significant )

https://drive.google.com/
open?id=1tMzybVvl3RuIQWCylWJI5wi-VWO07Yw6
Ruth Lalmuanzuali

Customer Perception of Quality: Importance and Factors
Influencing It

https://drive.google.com/
open?id=1HM1A83OhZyXrRQ4Q3FQcKhv2VFOf3CB5
Sanglianmawii Pachuau

Impact of market segmentation on resorts profitability

https://drive.google.com/
open?id=1d8iR1GZ4hvPrgSxTT2waggK6fo92iBaJ
Lalbiaknungi

Dimensions of product and service quality

https://drive.google.com/
open?id=1fiOLzFu_dNrTVWUCPfUt3u3k9-DSsaf9
PC. Zomuansanga

Understanding the 8D Methodology for Problem Solving

https://drive.google.com/
open?id=1ZEUAhRpRBayX7c5_IDzcx0bnVSG2Hk8a
Lalkaisangi

Contributions of Masaaki Imai to Quality Management

https://drive.google.com/
open?id=1ZYlfWJoTPU4lnVKvr1SeO1evMqRrNPGE

J. Lalremtluanga

Translating Customer Needs into Requirements

https://drive.google.com/
open?id=1XMQf4VaHHq75Hq5Nvz8vjai9VRJDDK0n

Ismael Lalduhsaka

Consumer Focus in Quality Management

https://drive.google.com/
open?id=113R2ostwKktacSXMEhjBonn7Zp6C4DRA
Rohit Kumar Rajak

TQM, Benefits of Implementing Total Quality Management

https://drive.google.com/
open?id=1nsdGMK6x4wZa1LbpJwLmvuisaQudFEgN
Sanglianmawii Pachuau

Quality planning Importance and process

https://drive.google.com/
open?id=1yDoBcoKyyvnFE2gTuEDmfTfp5XLpYixI
Rony Lalchhuanawma

Vision statement importance and components

https://drive.google.com/
open?id=1zVl4icGADAMunPkSDwuHVuzWqhpIN3N8
**Previous Year Exam Paper**
CAE 308 Food Quality Management Final Exam QP Set-1
https://foodqulaitymanagement.blogspot.com/2024/04/
food-quality-management-book-table-of.html

CAE 308 Food Quality Management Final Exam QP Set-1

CAE 308 Food Quality Management Final Exam QP Set 2
https://foodqulaitymanagement.blogspot.com/2024/04/
FQM2.html

CAE 308 Food Quality Management Final Exam QP Set 2

Quality Management Service MBATH/2/FC/04 Set 1

https://foodqulaitymanagement.blogspot.com/2024/04/QMSset1.html

Quality Management Service MBATH Set 1

Quality Management Service MBATH/2/FC/04 Set 2
https://foodqulaitymanagement.blogspot.com/2024/04/QMS1.html

Quality Managemsent Service MBATH Set 2

Midterm Exam Quality Management Set 1
https://foodqulaitymanagement.blogspot.com/2024/04/
midQMS2.html

Midterm Exam Quality Management Set 1

Midterm Exam Quality Management Set 2
https://foodqulaitymanagement.blogspot.com/2024/04/
midQMS2_01691895960.html

Midterm Exam Quality Management Set 2

156

# References


1. AOAC International. (2021). Official Methods of Analysis of AOAC INTERNATIONAL.
2. AMSA. (2020). Meat Color Measurement Guidelines.
3. Buzby, J. C., & Unnevehr, L. J. (2018). Food safety and international trade. In The Oxford Handbook of Food, Politics, and Society. Oxford University Press.
4. Caswell, J. A., & Hooker, N. H. (1996). HACCP as an international trade standard. American Journal of Agricultural Economics, 78(3), 775–779.
5. Charlebois, S., & Summan, A. (2015). Food fraud: An exploratory study for measuring consumer perceptions towards mislabeled food products and their influence on self-authentication intentions. Trends in Food Science & Technology, 45(2), 211–218.
6. Codex Alimentarius Commission. (2003). Codex Alimentarius: General principles of food hygiene. FAO/WHO.
7. Codex Alimentarius Commission. (2019). Hazard Analysis and Critical Control Point (HACCP) System and Guidelines for its Application.
8. Codex Alimentarius Commission. (2020). General Principles of Food Hygiene.
9. Codex Alimentarius Commission. (2003). Code of hygienic practice for milk and milk products. FAO.
10. Crosby, P. B. (1979). Quality is free: The art of making quality certain. McGraw-Hill.
11. Deming, W. E. (1986). Out of the crisis. MIT Press.
12. Directorate of Marketing and Inspection. (1937). Agricultural Produce (Grading and Marketing) Act, 1937. DMI.
13. Evans, J. R., & Lindsay, W. M. (2017). Managing for quality and performance excellence. Cengage Learning.
14. European Commission. (2018). Food Quality and Safety.

15. European Commission. (2019). EU Food Traceability System.

16. FDA. (2021). Food Safety Modernization Act (FSMA).

17. FDA. (2021). Food Labeling Guide.

18. Federal Food, Drug, and Cosmetic Act, 21 U.S.C. § 301 et seq. (1938).

19. Feigenbaum, A. V. (1991). Total quality control. McGraw-Hill.

20. Food and Agriculture Organization. (1997). Quality and quality changes in fresh fish. FAO fisheries technical paper, (348).

21. Food and Agriculture Organization. (2003). Good Agricultural Practices (GAP) on horticultural production for extension staff in Tanzania. FAO.

22. Food and Agriculture Organization & World Health Organization. (1963). Codex Alimentarius. FAO.

23. Food Safety and Standards Authority of India. (2006). Food Safety and Standards Act, 2006. FSSAI.

24. Garcia-Gonzalez, D. L., & Sun, D. W. (Eds.). (2010). Near-Infrared Spectroscopy in Food Science and Technology. Wiley-Blackwell.

25. Garvin, D. A. (1984). What does "product quality" really mean? Sloan Management Review, 26(1), 25–43.

26. Garvin, D. A. (1987). Competing on the eight dimensions of quality. Harvard Business Review, 65(6), 101–109.

27. Goetsch, D. L., & Davis, S. B. (2014). Quality management for organizational excellence. Pearson.

28. GS1. (2021). Traceability Guidelines for Fresh Produce.

29. Handfield, R. B., & Nichols, E. L. (1999). Introduction to Supply Chain Management. Prentice Hall.

30. Herzberg, F. (2003). One more time: How do you motivate employees? Harvard Business Review Press. (Original work published 1968)

31. Imai, M. (1986). Kaizen: The Key to Japan's Competitive Success. McGraw-Hill.

32. Institute of Food Technologists (IFT). (2017). Sampling and Testing Methods for Food Safety.

33. International Organization for Standardization. (2005). ISO

22000: 2005. Food safety management systems-Requirements for any organization in the food chain. ISO.

34. International Organization for Standardization (ISO). (2021). ISO 22000 - Food Safety Management.

35. ISO. (2018). ISO 9001:2015 Quality management systems – Requirements.

36. Ishikawa, K. (1985). What is total quality control? The Japanese way. Prentice-Hall.

37. Ishikawa, K., & Loftus, J. H. (1985). Introduction to quality control. 3A Corporation.

38. Jay, J. M., Loessner, M. J., & Golden, D. A. (2005). Modern food microbiology. Springer.

39. Johnson, R. W., & Patel, N. K. (2018). Artificial Intelligence in the Food Industry: Challenges and Perspectives. Springer.

40. Jones, A. (2017). Sustainable food production and ethics. Preprints.

41. Juran, J. M. (1992). Juran on quality by design: The new steps for planning quality into goods and services. Free Press.

42. Juran, J. M., & Godfrey, A. B. (Eds.). (1999). Juran's quality handbook (5th ed.). McGraw-Hill.

43. Kamilaris, A., Fonts, A., & Prenafeta-Boldú, F. X. (2019). The rise of blockchain technology in agriculture and food supply chains. Trends in Food Science & Technology, 91, 640–652.

44. Lawless, H. T., & Heymann, H. (2010). Sensory evaluation of food: principles and practices. Springer Science & Business Media.

45. Lelieveld, H. L. M., Mostert, M. A., & Holah, J. (2014). Handbook of hygiene control in the food industry. Woodhead Publishing.

46. Lencioni, P. (2002). The five dysfunctions of a team: A leadership fable. Jossey-Bass.

47. Manning, L., & Soon, J. M. (2016). Food safety, food fraud, and food defense: a fast evolving literature. Journal of Food Science, 81(4), R823–R834.

48. Margeirsson, B., Lauzon, H. L., Margeirsson, S., & Martinsdóttir, E. (2011). Traceability in the Icelandic cod value chain. Journal

of Food Science, 76(8), S386–S396.

49. Meilgaard, M. C., Civille, G. V., & Carr, B. T. (2006). Sensory evaluation techniques. CRC Press.

50. Ministry of Consumer Affairs, Food and Public Distribution. (1955). The Essential Commodities Act, 1955. Government of India.

51. Monczka, R. M., Handfield, R. B., & Giunipero, L. C. (2016). Purchasing and Supply Chain Management. Cengage Learning.

52. Montgomery, D. C. (2017). Introduction to Statistical Quality Control. John Wiley & Sons.

53. Mortimore, S., & Wallace, C. (2013). HACCP: A practical approach. Springer.

54. Oakland, J. S. (2003). Total quality management: text with cases. Butterworth-Heinemann.

55. Oakland, J. S. (2014). Total Quality Management and Operational Excellence: Text with Cases. Routledge.

56. O'Donnell, C. P. (2019). Challenges in Food Quality Assurance. Comprehensive Reviews in Food Science and Food Safety, 18(5), 1412–1432.

57. Oakley, E. (2017). Principles of Food Quality Assurance. Journal of Food Science, 20(4), 102–115.

58. Pyzdek, T., & Keller, P. A. (2018). The Six Sigma handbook (5th ed.). McGraw-Hill.

59. Senge, P. M. (1990). The Fifth Discipline: The Art & Practice of The Learning Organization. Doubleday.

60. Shingo, S. (1988). Non-Stock Production: The Shingo System of Continuous Improvement. Productivity Press.

61. Sivakumar, A. I., & Palaniappan, M. (2012). Statistical methods for textile technologists. Woodhead Publishing India Pvt. Ltd.

62. Smith, A. B., & Johnson, C. D. (2021). Biosensors in Food Processing. Springer.

63. Smith, J. (2019). Understanding Food Quality. Food Science Journal, 15(2), 45–60.

64. Sperber, W. H., & Stier, R. F. (2009). Happy 50th birthday to HACCP: Retrospective and prospective. Food Control, 20(2),

94–97.

65. Stone, H., & Sidel, J. L. (2004). Sensory evaluation practices. Elsevier.

66. Summers, D. C. (2005). Quality (5$^{th}$ ed.). Prentice Hall.

67. Sun, D. W. (2014). Emerging technologies for food processing. Academic Press.

68. Sunil Kumar. (2023). A textbook on Culinary Education. Notion Press.

69. Surak, J. G. (2008). A recipe for safe food: ISO 22000 and HACCP. Quality Progress, 41(8), 45–50.

70. Tao, Y., & Sun, D. W. (2014). Advanced Applications of Near-Infrared Spectroscopy in Food Analysis. CRC Press.

71. U.S. Food and Drug Administration. (2017). FSMA final rule on foreign supplier verification programs (FSVP) for importers of food for humans and animals.

72. U.S. Food and Drug Administration (FDA). (2018). Current Good Manufacturing Practice (CGMP) Regulations.

73. U.S. Food and Drug Administration (FDA). (2021). Food Labeling Guide.

74. USDA Agricultural Marketing Service. (2020). National Organic Program.

75. Wang, Y., & Yu, H. (2020). Food Fraud Detection and Prevention: Techniques and Strategies. Wiley.

76. World Health Organization. (2006). Five keys to safer food manual.

77. World Health Organization. (2015). WHO estimates the global burden of foodborne diseases: foodborne disease burden epidemiology reference group 2007–2015.

78. World Health Organization 1 (WHO). (2020). Good Manufacturing Practices for Pharmaceuticals.

79. https://foodqulaitymanagement.blogspot.com/

# Other Book Published By Dr Sunil Kumar

Book Are Available on Amazon & Filpcart

Book Are Available on Amazon & Filpcart

www.ingramcontent.com/pod-product-compliance
Lightning Source LLC
Chambersburg PA
CBHW040807110726
47973CB00009B/130